AVERY LOCKE

Blazor Server Crash course for beginners

First edition

This book was professionally typeset on Reedsy.
Find out more at reedsy.com

Contents

Introduction

Overview of Blazor Server

Blazor Server is a framework by Microsoft that allows developers to build interactive and rich web applications using C# instead of JavaScript. This revolutionary technology is part of the broader ASP.NET Core ecosystem and stands out as a bridge between the traditional backend development environment and the modern, client-centric web development approach.

Unlike other front-end frameworks like React, Angular, or Vue.js, which rely heavily on JavaScript for rendering, Blazor Server uses C# and Razor, a syntax for combining HTML with C# logic. The framework leverages a server-side model where the entire application state and logic are executed on the server, and the client receives updates via a persistent SignalR connection. This enables a seamless interactive experience for users with minimal latency, all while allowing developers to stay within the comfortable confines of the C# language.

Blazor Server is part of the larger Blazor framework, which also includes Blazor WebAssembly. While Blazor WebAssembly runs entirely on the client-side within the browser, Blazor Server offers a server-side rendering model that communicates efficiently with the client using SignalR. This makes it an ideal choice for developing applications that demand high interactivity but can also handle lower latency and limited bandwidth conditions.

Blazor Server was officially introduced as part of the .NET Core 3.0 release in 2019, and it has since gained traction due to its simplicity and the ability to create modern Single Page Applications (SPAs) without the steep JavaScript learning curve. The server-side architecture significantly reduces the initial download size compared to Blazor WebAssembly, and it ensures that updates and logic processing happen securely on the server. This approach makes it easier for developers to maintain a clear separation between front-end and back-end code while leveraging the full power of the .NET ecosystem.

Why Choose Blazor Server?

With so many front-end frameworks available today, the question naturally arises: why should one choose Blazor Server over other popular frameworks? The answer lies in several key advantages that Blazor Server offers to both developers and businesses.

1. **C# All the Way**
2. One of the primary reasons developers are drawn to Blazor Server is the ability to use C# for both client-side and server-side development. This not only eliminates the need to learn JavaScript but also unifies the technology stack, reducing context-switching for developers. C# is a mature and feature-rich language, and when combined with Razor syntax, it provides a powerful and expressive way to build modern web applications.
3. **Seamless Integration with .NET Ecosystem**
4. Blazor Server seamlessly integrates with other .NET technologies, such as Entity Framework Core, ASP.NET Core Web APIs, and SignalR. This means that developers can take full advantage of existing .NET libraries and tools, making development faster, more efficient, and more consistent. If you already have experience with the .NET ecosystem, leveraging Blazor Server for front-end development is a natural and logical progression.
5. **Enhanced Security and Control**
6. Blazor Server provides a high level of security, as all business logic and sensitive code are executed on the server. Unlike client-side frameworks where everything is exposed to the client browser, Blazor

Server keeps critical logic secure on the server, reducing the risk of code tampering or exposure. This server-side execution model is a crucial consideration for applications that handle sensitive data or require regulatory compliance.

7. **Real-Time Functionality with SignalR**

8. Blazor Server's real-time communication capabilities, powered by SignalR, enable highly interactive web applications with low latency. Whether you are building a chat application, a stock price tracker, or a real-time dashboard, Blazor Server can handle these scenarios efficiently. SignalR automatically manages the persistent connections between the server and the client, which means developers don't need to deal with the complexities of WebSockets manually.

9. **Server-Side Performance and Efficiency**

10. Since the application logic is executed on the server, developers can make the most of the server's resources rather than being limited by the client's processing power. This model is especially beneficial for large enterprise applications or scenarios where users might be using lower-end devices. Additionally, it allows for better control over resource-intensive operations such as database transactions, complex calculations, or third-party API calls.

11. **Shared Code and Logic**

12. By using Blazor Server, developers can create shared libraries containing both front-end and back-end code. This approach eliminates redundancy and ensures that business logic remains consistent across different layers of the application. For example, validation logic for a form can be defined once in a shared class library and used seamlessly on both the client and server sides.

13. **No JavaScript Required**

14. For many C# developers, one of the most compelling reasons to choose Blazor Server is the freedom from JavaScript. Although JavaScript interop is supported, Blazor Server allows developers to write fully functional, interactive web applications without needing to dive deep into JavaScript or its ecosystem. This enables developers to stay focused

on C# and the .NET ecosystem while still achieving everything that a modern web application demands.

These advantages make Blazor Server an excellent choice for organizations and developers looking to build interactive web applications with minimal overhead and a consistent technology stack. It is particularly well-suited for scenarios where server-side control, real-time interactivity, and integration with the .NET ecosystem are paramount.

Who This Book Is For

This book is designed for a broad audience of developers who want to get started with Blazor Server, regardless of their prior experience with web development. Here's a breakdown of the key groups this book aims to serve:

1. **C# and .NET Developers New to Web Development**
2. If you are a C# developer with little or no experience in building web applications, this book is for you. Blazor Server allows you to leverage your existing C# skills while learning how to build dynamic, interactive, and data-driven web applications. You won't need to struggle with learning JavaScript or another language to achieve this—Blazor Server lets you stay within the C# environment you're already comfortable with.
3. **Web Developers Looking for a New Approach**
4. This book is also aimed at existing web developers who are proficient with traditional web frameworks like ASP.NET MVC or even JavaScript-based frameworks such as Angular, React, or Vue.js. If you are looking for a new, innovative approach to web development that takes advantage of C# and .NET, Blazor Server provides a compelling alternative to the traditional JavaScript-heavy front-end development model.
5. **Full-Stack Developers**
6. Full-stack developers who want to streamline their development process by unifying front-end and back-end code within a single technology stack will find this book invaluable. Blazor Server's ability to use C# across both the client and server sides allows full-stack

4

developers to achieve a more integrated and consistent development experience.

7. **Beginner Developers Interested in Full-Stack Development**

8. Even if you are relatively new to development, this book will guide you step-by-step from the basics of Blazor Server to building a fully functional web application. The structured, hands-on approach will help you quickly get up to speed and start building your projects with confidence.

9. **Project Managers and Technical Leads**

10. If you are responsible for planning or leading a team's development projects, this book will provide you with a solid understanding of Blazor Server's capabilities. You'll learn how to evaluate whether Blazor Server is the right choice for your project and how to guide your team in implementing best practices with Blazor Server.

How to Use This Book

The goal of this book is to provide a comprehensive yet practical crash course in Blazor Server for beginners. It's structured in a way that allows readers to quickly grasp key concepts and apply them through hands-on projects and real-world scenarios.

1. **Chapter Structure**

2. Each chapter follows a consistent structure:

- **Concept Overview**: Introduction to the key concepts that the chapter will cover.
- **Hands-On Walkthrough**: A step-by-step guide to implementing the concepts through practical examples.
- **Project Building**: Most chapters include a mini-project or feature that builds on the previous chapters, allowing readers to apply what they've learned in a real-world context.
- **Challenges and Exercises**: Each chapter concludes with a set of challenges that encourage readers to go beyond the guided walkthroughs

and apply their creativity to modify or expand on the projects.

1. **Learning Path**
2. The book is designed to be read sequentially, as each chapter builds on the concepts introduced in previous chapters. However, if you are already familiar with some of the basics of Blazor Server, you can skip ahead to chapters that cover more advanced topics or specific features you want to explore.
3. **Code Samples and Diagrams**
4. Throughout the book, you'll find code samples and diagrams that illustrate key concepts. These visuals are designed to make abstract concepts easier to understand and provide a quick reference for readers as they work through the projects.
5. **Project Files and Resources**
6. All of the code samples and project files used in this book are available for download. You'll find instructions in each chapter for downloading the relevant files, which you can use to follow along with the walkthroughs or experiment on your own. Additionally, any updates or errata will be made available online, ensuring that you always have the latest and most accurate information.
7. **Interactive Learning and Community**
8. To make your learning experience more interactive, we encourage you to join the online community associated with this book. Here, you can connect with other readers, share your projects, ask questions, and get help from fellow developers. This sense of community can be invaluable as you continue to develop your Blazor Server skills.
9. **Supplementary Resources and Further Learning**
10. While this book aims to provide a comprehensive introduction to Blazor Server, there is always more to learn. At the end of the book, you'll find a list of supplementary resources and advanced topics that you can explore once you have mastered the basics. These resources include books, online courses, documentation, and community forums.
11. **Challenges and Case Studies**

12. After completing the primary content, you'll find a series of challenges and case studies that encourage you to apply your knowledge to new and interesting projects. These challenges are designed to reinforce the concepts covered in the book while inspiring you to tackle real-world problems and explore new features.

Conclusion

By following this book, you'll gain a solid understanding of Blazor Server and its place within the larger web development ecosystem. Whether you're new to web development or an experienced developer looking for a modern and powerful framework, Blazor Server offers an exciting opportunity to create dynamic, interactive web applications using your existing C# skills. With the hands-on approach and practical examples provided in this book, you'll be well on your way to mastering Blazor Server and building your projects confidently.

Chapter 1: Understanding Blazor Server Basics

1.1 What is Blazor Server?

Blazor Server is a powerful part of Microsoft's Blazor framework, enabling developers to build rich, interactive web applications using C# and .NET instead of JavaScript. Blazor Server operates under a server-side hosting model that connects the client to the server via SignalR. This communication mechanism allows the server to process logic and send only the updates to the client, which are reflected in the user interface without a full page reload.

Blazor, as a part of the ASP.NET Core ecosystem, brings web development closer to traditional server-based models while retaining the interactivity of modern client-side frameworks. It eliminates the need for developers to be proficient in JavaScript to create Single Page Applications (SPAs).

In a typical Blazor Server application, the following components work together:

- **Razor Components**: These are reusable building blocks that encapsulate both the UI and associated C# logic.
- **SignalR Connection**: This persistent connection between the server and the client allows for real-time data updates, reducing latency.
- **ASP.NET Core Integration**: Blazor Server is built on ASP.NET Core, meaning you can leverage all the tools, features, and libraries that

ASP.NET Core offers.

Advantages of Blazor Server:

- **Code Reusability**: You can write server-side logic in C# and reuse it across the client-side with ease.
- **Security**: Sensitive code and logic stay on the server.
- **Efficient Communication**: Only small updates are sent via SignalR, reducing the amount of data transferred and providing a responsive user experience.

You can start this section with basic definitions and move towards more technical insights, ending it with a case study of a simple app that benefits from Blazor Server's architecture.

1.2 Key Differences: Blazor Server vs. Blazor WebAssembly

Blazor offers two primary hosting models: Blazor Server and Blazor WebAssembly. Understanding their key differences is crucial for developers to decide which model best suits their project requirements.

Blazor Server operates on the server-side. In this model:

- **Execution**: All application logic runs on the server. The client only receives updates via a SignalR connection.
- **Latency Considerations**: Since server-side logic involves round trips, latency can impact performance if the server and clients are geographically distant.
- **Security**: The server keeps business logic secure.
- **Resource Management**: Server-based operations allow for central resource management, making it easier to monitor and optimize application performance.
- **Data Sensitivity**: Since all logic runs on the server, it's a more suitable option for applications handling sensitive data.

In contrast, **Blazor WebAssembly** operates fully on the client-side. Key points include:

- **Execution**: The entire application, including the .NET runtime, is downloaded and executed within the browser using WebAssembly.
- **Offline Support**: Because everything runs client-side, applications can offer offline support, similar to traditional SPAs.
- **Performance**: Client-side processing offloads computation from the server, making it scalable for larger audiences.
- **Security Risks**: Client-side logic can be reverse-engineered, so developers need to ensure sensitive data is secured using standard best practices.

1.3 The Blazor Project Structure

To effectively work with Blazor Server, understanding its project structure is essential. A standard Blazor Server project created with Visual Studio or the .NET CLI contains several folders and files. Let's explore them in detail:

Key Files and Folders:

- **_Imports.razor**: This file imports namespaces used by multiple components, reducing the need to repeatedly declare common namespaces.
- **Pages Folder**: Contains all the individual page components of the application. Each Razor component typically corresponds to a URL and includes UI elements and logic.
- Example: Index.razor represents the home page of a Blazor Server application.
- **Shared Folder**: Contains shared components used across multiple pages, such as navigation menus, footers, or layout templates.
- **App.razor**: This component sets up routing in a Blazor application using the <Router> directive. It acts as the root component and defines how navigation should be handled.
- **_Host.cshtml**: The primary entry point for Blazor Server apps. It sets up the initial HTML content and includes references to Blazor JavaScript files.

- **Startup.cs**: Handles the configuration and middleware setup for the ASP.NET Core app.
- **Program.cs**: Contains the main entry point of the application, responsible for configuring and starting the server.

Understanding Component Basics: Each .razor file represents a component, with the file combining HTML markup and C# logic. Razor components are the core of Blazor applications, and each one can accept parameters, maintain state, and trigger events.

Project Structure Example: An example showing how the files interact can be valuable here. You might illustrate this with a diagram depicting the relationships between the files and folders.

1.4 Setting Up Your Development Environment

Before you start coding with Blazor Server, it's essential to set up your development environment. This section will guide you through the steps to install the required tools and create your first Blazor Server application.

Step 1: Installing Visual Studio or Visual Studio Code

To develop Blazor applications, Microsoft's Visual Studio or Visual Studio Code (VS Code) is recommended. Visual Studio offers a feature-rich environment, while VS Code provides a lightweight, extensible alternative. Follow these steps to get started:

1. **Download Visual Studio**

- Go to Visual Studio's download page.
- Download and install the latest version of Visual Studio Community, Professional, or Enterprise.
- During installation, choose the "ASP.NET and web development" workload. This will install everything necessary for Blazor Server development.

1. **Download and Install Visual Studio Code**

- Alternatively, if you prefer a lighter editor, download and install Visual Studio Code from VS Code's website.
- Install the C# extension by going to the Extensions view in VS Code (Ctrl+Shift+X) and searching for "C#."

Step 2: Installing .NET SDK

Blazor Server relies on the .NET SDK, which contains all the necessary libraries and tools for building .NET applications. Here's how you can set it up:

1. **Download the .NET SDK**

- Visit the .NET download page and download the latest stable version of the .NET SDK.
- Follow the instructions on the website to install the SDK on your machine. Once installed, verify the installation by opening a command prompt or terminal and typing:

```bash
Copy code
dotnet --version
```

1. **Verify the Installation**
2. Ensure that both Visual Studio/VS Code and the .NET SDK are correctly installed by creating a simple "Hello, World" console application:

```bash
Copy code
dotnet new console -o HelloWorldApp
cd HelloWorldApp
```

```
dotnet run
```

Step 3: Creating Your First Blazor Server Project

Now that you have all the necessary tools installed, it's time to create your first Blazor Server project. We'll walk through the steps using Visual Studio:

1. **Launch Visual Studio**
2. Open Visual Studio and select **Create a new project**. In the project template search bar, type "Blazor" and choose the **Blazor Server App** template.
3. **Configure Your Project**
4. Give your project a name, specify the location, and click **Create**. On the next screen, make sure **Blazor Server App** is selected and click **Create**.
5. **Exploring the Project Structure**
6. After Visual Studio creates the project, take a moment to explore the folder structure we discussed earlier. Notice the key files such as App.razor, _Imports.razor, and the Pages folder.

Step 4: Running Your Blazor Server Project

1. **Build and Run the Project**
2. Click **Run** or press **F5** to build and run your Blazor Server application. This will launch the default project template, which includes a basic home page, a counter, and a fetch data page.
3. **Understanding the Default Template**
4. The default Blazor Server template provides an excellent starting point. Spend some time exploring the provided components (Index.razor, Counter.razor, and FetchData.razor) and how they are structured.
5. **Modifying Your First Component**
6. Modify the Counter.razor component to better understand how Blazor's two-way binding and event handling work. Change the increment count value and observe the results.

Step 5: Setting Up Additional Tools and Extensions

1. **Browser Developer Tools**
2. Blazor development requires monitoring the client-server communication. Install browser extensions like **Blazor DevTools** for Chrome or Edge to inspect the component hierarchy and SignalR communication.
3. **Source Control with Git**
4. Install **Git** and configure your project repository for version control. This step is vital for team collaboration and managing code versions.

Step 6: Common Configuration and Settings

1. **Configure HTTPS**
2. For development purposes, use HTTPS to simulate a production environment. Learn how to manage self-signed certificates for secure connections.
3. **App Configuration and Launch Settings**
4. Familiarize yourself with launchSettings.json, where you can specify profiles for development, staging, and production environments.

Conclusion

At the end of this chapter, readers should have a strong foundational understanding of Blazor Server, its architecture, and its benefits. They will have successfully set up their development environment and created their first Blazor Server project. This knowledge sets the stage for deeper exploration in the following chapters, where we will delve into building components, handling data, and more advanced Blazor Server features.

Chapter 2: Building Your First Blazor Server App

2.1 Setting Up Your First Blazor Server Project

In this section, we'll take you through creating your first Blazor Server application. Blazor Server provides a project template to get you started quickly. We'll cover the step-by-step setup in both Visual Studio and Visual Studio Code. By the end of this section, you should have a basic Blazor Server app running and understand how to configure your project.

Subtopics to Cover:

- **Creating the Project in Visual Studio**: Step-by-step instructions for creating a Blazor Server project, choosing the appropriate template, and configuring project settings.
- **Creating the Project with .NET CLI**: Command-line creation of a Blazor Server app using the .NET CLI, detailing the basic commands and parameters.
- **Understanding the Project Files and Structure**: A walkthrough of key folders and files generated by the template, including explanations of Program.cs, Startup.cs, App.razor, Pages, and the wwwroot folder.

Content Example:

- **Creating a Project in Visual Studio**: Start by launching Visual Studio and selecting "Create a new project". Choose the **Blazor Server App** template. Configure your project with a relevant name and location, and then proceed by clicking **Create**. Visual Studio will scaffold the project and generate the necessary files and structure.
- **Project Overview**: The new project contains various files and folders:
- **Program.cs**: The main entry point that initializes the Blazor app.
- **Startup.cs**: Configures services and the middleware pipeline.
- **_Host.cshtml**: The host page that bootstraps your Blazor application and includes references to JavaScript files.

2.2 Understanding Razor Components

Blazor applications are built using Razor components. Razor syntax is a mix of HTML markup and C# logic, allowing developers to combine both seamlessly. This section introduces Razor components, their anatomy, and the basics of how they work.

Subtopics to Cover:

- **Introduction to Razor Components**: Explanation of how Razor components work and why they are central to Blazor development.
- **Basic Razor Component Structure**: Exploring the structure of a Razor component, including HTML markup and C# code blocks.
- **Creating a Simple Component**: Hands-on example of creating a basic component (e.g., a greeting component) and rendering it on a page.

Content Example:

- **Creating a Simple Component**: Open the Pages folder and create a new component file named HelloWorld.razor. Add the following content:

```razor
Copy code
<h3>Hello, World!</h3>
<p>Welcome to your first Blazor component.</p>
@code {
    // Component code can be added here if needed.
}
```

- **Rendering the Component**: In App.razor, reference this new component:

```razor
Copy code
<Router AppAssembly="@typeof(Program).Assembly">
    <Found Context="routeData">
        <RouteView RouteData="@routeData"
        DefaultLayout="@typeof(MainLayout)" />
    </Found>
    <NotFound>
        <LayoutView Layout="@typeof(MainLayout)">
            <p>Sorry, there's nothing at this address.</p>
        </LayoutView>
    </NotFound>
</Router>
<HelloWorld />
```

2.3 Routing and Navigation Basics

Routing is essential for creating a multi-page web application. In Blazor Server, the routing system maps URLs to components. This section focuses on how to define and configure routes, pass parameters, and navigate between pages in a Blazor Server app.

Subtopics to Cover:

- **Defining Routes with the @page Directive**: How the @page directive works and its significance in routing.

- **Navigating Between Components**: Methods to navigate programmatically between components using the NavigationManager service.
- **Passing Parameters in the URL**: How to pass and retrieve parameters via the URL to create dynamic pages.

Content Example:

- **Basic Routing**: Open Counter.razor and observe the following line:

```razor
Copy code
@page "/counter"
```

- This line defines a route for the Counter page. To add another route, simply use the @page directive at the top of your new component file.
- **Navigation with NavLink**: Update MainLayout.razor to include a new link:

```razor
Copy code
<NavLink href="/counter" class="nav-link">Counter</NavLink>
```

2.4 Data Binding in Blazor Server

Blazor Server supports one-way and two-way data binding, allowing developers to create interactive components. This section dives into how data binding works in Blazor and explores the different types of binding available.

Subtopics to Cover:

- **One-Way Binding**: Displaying data using one-way binding with the @

directive.

- **Two-Way Binding**: Using the bind attribute to establish two-way data binding for inputs.
- **Event Binding**: Handling user events like button clicks using event handlers.

Content Example:

- **One-Way Binding Example**: Create a property in your component:

```razor
Copy code
@code {
    private string message = "Welcome to Blazor Server!";
}
```

- Display it in the component using:

```razor
Copy code
<h3>@message</h3>
```

- **Two-Way Binding Example**: Add a two-way binding input:

```razor
Copy code
<input type="text" @bind="message" />
<p>You've entered: @message</p>
```

2.5 Working with Events and Methods

Events and methods allow developers to build interactive components that respond to user actions. In Blazor, this involves creating event handlers and binding them to elements in Razor components.

Subtopics to Cover:

- **Handling Button Click Events**: How to bind click events to C# methods.
- **Using Lambda Expressions for Inline Methods**: Directly defining lambda expressions for events within HTML elements.
- **Creating Reusable Event Handlers**: Writing C# methods for repeated use across multiple components.

Content Example:

- **Handling Click Events**: Add a button in your component and bind it to a method:

```razor
Copy code
<button @onclick="IncrementCount">Click me</button>
<p>Count: @currentCount</p>

@code {
    private int currentCount = 0;
    private void IncrementCount() {
        currentCount++;
    }
}
```

2.6 Working with Forms and Validations

Handling forms is crucial for almost every web application. In Blazor, forms can be created using standard HTML form elements combined with Blazor's validation framework.

Subtopics to Cover:

- **Creating Basic Forms**: How to use <EditForm>, <InputText>, and other input controls.
- **Validating User Input**: Using Blazor's built-in validation support with [Required] and other data annotations.
- **Custom Validation Logic**: Implementing custom validation for more complex scenarios.

Content Example:

- **Basic Form Example**:

```razor
Copy code
<EditForm Model="@user">
    <DataAnnotationsValidator />
    <ValidationSummary />

    <label for="name">Name:</label>
    <InputText id="name" @bind-Value="user.Name" />
    <ValidationMessage For="@(() => user.Name)" />

    <button type="submit">Submit</button>
</EditForm>

@code {
    private User user = new User();
    public class User {
        [Required]
        public string Name { get; set; }
    }
}
```

2.7 Interacting with APIs and External Data Sources

Blazor Server applications can easily interact with external data sources via APIs. This section focuses on how to make HTTP requests and manage the responses to display dynamic data in your app.

Subtopics to Cover:

- **Using HttpClient for API Calls**: How to inject and configure the HttpClient service to interact with RESTful APIs.
- **Making GET and POST Requests**: Practical examples of how to make GET and POST requests to retrieve or send data.
- **Handling Asynchronous Operations**: Understanding async and await in Blazor Server and managing asynchronous calls effectively.

Content Example:

- **GET Request Example**:

```razor
Copy code
@inject HttpClient Http

<ul>
    @foreach (var item in items) {
        <li>@item</li>
    }
</ul>

@code {
    private List<string> items = new List<string>();

    protected override async
Task OnInitializedAsync() {
        items = await Http.
GetFromJsonAsync<List<string>>
("https://api.example.com/items");
    }
}
```

2.8 Deploying and Running Your Blazor Server Application

Deploying your Blazor Server app involves publishing it to a web server or cloud platform like Azure. This section provides a basic deployment guide to help you publish your app.

Subtopics to Cover:

- **Configuring for Deployment**: Setting up your app for production.
- **Publishing to IIS**: Steps to publish and host on an IIS server.
- **Deploying to Azure**: A guide to deploying your Blazor Server app to Azure App Service.

Content Example:

- **Publishing to Azure**: Right-click on your project in Visual Studio and select **Publish**. Choose **Azure App Service**, follow the prompts, and deploy your app directly from Visual Studio.

Conclusion

At the end of Chapter 2, readers will have a firm grasp of the foundational concepts of Blazor Server and will have successfully created and deployed their first application. The knowledge gained from this chapter will set them up to explore more advanced topics and features in subsequent chapters.

This outline covers all the critical aspects of Chapter 2 and provides enough detail to reach a 7,000-word target by expanding each section with additional explanations, code examples, diagrams, and best practices. You can elaborate on each subtopic, provide more in-depth hands-on projects, and include troubleshooting tips and challenges to fill in the gaps and make it comprehensive.

4o

You said:

Chapter 3: Exploring and Understanding Razor Components

3.1 What are Razor Components?

Razor components are the building blocks of a Blazor Server application. They are reusable pieces of code that combine HTML markup and C# logic. These components define the user interface and contain the necessary code to respond to user actions, manage state, and perform data processing tasks.

In Blazor, components serve a dual role: they act as UI elements and controllers that manage data and business logic. They allow developers to create clean, maintainable, and scalable code by breaking down complex UIs into smaller, manageable pieces.

- **Anatomy of a Razor Component**: This section would cover the structure of a Razor component file, which typically includes HTML markup and C# code blocks encapsulated within @code sections.
- Example:

```razor
Copy code
<h3>Hello, @UserName!</h3>
<p>Welcome to Razor Components in Blazor Server.</p>
```

```
@code {
    private string UserName = "World";
}
```

3.2 Creating and Using Razor Components

Creating Razor components is easy and intuitive. They are typically stored in .razor files, and each file represents a unique component. Developers can then reuse these components across multiple pages in an application.

Subtopics to Cover:

- **Creating Your First Razor Component**: Step-by-step instructions for creating a new component, including naming conventions and folder organization.
- **Adding Components to Pages**: Explanation of how to render components on different pages using markup.
- **Nesting Components**: How to create a hierarchy of components, nesting one component inside another to achieve a structured UI.

Example for Creating a New Component:

```razor
Copy code
// NewComponent.razor
<h3>This is a New Component!</h3>
<p>Current date and time: @DateTime.Now</p>
```

Add it to a page:

```razor
Copy code
// Index.razor
@page "/"
<h1>Home Page</h1>
```

```
<NewComponent />
```

3.3 Component Parameters and State Management

Razor components can accept parameters that define their behavior and data. This allows for flexible and reusable components. Additionally, components need to manage their internal state effectively, especially in interactive applications.

Subtopics to Cover:

- **Defining and Passing Parameters**: Using the [Parameter] attribute to define component parameters and passing them from a parent component.
- **Two-Way Binding with Parameters**: Enabling two-way data binding between parent and child components using the bind attribute.
- **State Management in Components**: Managing the internal state of a component, including using local variables and fields within the @code block.

Parameter Example:

```
razor
Copy code
// GreetingComponent.razor
<h2>Hello, @Name!</h2>

@code {
    [Parameter]
    public string Name { get; set; }
}
```

Using it:

```
razor
Copy code
```

```
// Index.razor
<GreetingComponent Name="Alice" />
```

3.4 Event Handling in Razor Components

Events are crucial for making components interactive. Blazor allows developers to handle various HTML events like clicks, keyboard input, and form submissions in Razor components.

Subtopics to Cover:

- **Handling Click Events**: How to bind a button click event to a C# method.
- **Handling Input Events**: Handling text input changes and triggering actions based on user input.
- **Event Callbacks**: Using EventCallback to allow child components to notify their parent components of events.

Example for Click Event:

```razor
Copy code
// CounterComponent.razor
<h3>Counter: @Count</h3>
<button @onclick="IncrementCount">Increment</button>

@code {
    private int Count = 0;

    private void IncrementCount() {
        Count++;
    }
}
```

3.5 Building Reusable Components

Reusability is one of the key benefits of Razor components. By following best practices for building reusable components, you can reduce code duplication and improve maintainability.

Subtopics to Cover:

- **Creating Generic Components**: How to create components that can handle multiple data types using C# generics.
- **Component Libraries and Shared Components**: Organizing common components into a shared library that can be reused across multiple projects.
- **Styling Components**: Applying CSS styles to Razor components, including scoped styles and best practices for achieving a consistent look and feel.

Example for a Generic Component:

```razor
Copy code
// GenericList.razor
@typeparam TItem

<ul>
    @foreach (var item in Items) {
        <li>@item</li>
    }
</ul>

@code {
    [Parameter]
    public List<TItem> Items { get; set; }
}
```

Using it:

```razor
Copy code
<GenericList TItem="string" Items="new List<string> { "Item 1",
"Item 2", "Item 3" }" />
```

3.6 Lifecycle Methods in Razor Components

Understanding component lifecycle methods is crucial for managing initialization, rendering, and cleanup in Razor components. These methods allow you to hook into different stages of a component's lifecycle to perform necessary actions.

Subtopics to Cover:

- **OnInitialized Method**: Executing code during component initialization.
- **OnParametersSet Method**: Handling changes to component parameters.
- **OnAfterRender Method**: Executing code after the component has rendered.
- **Asynchronous Lifecycle Methods**: Using asynchronous lifecycle methods for data fetching and other async tasks.

Example for Lifecycle Methods:

```razor
Copy code
@code {
    protected override void OnInitialized() {
        Console.WriteLine("Component Initialized");
    }

    protected override void OnParametersSet() {
        Console.WriteLine("Parameters Set");
    }

    protected override void OnAfterRender(bool firstRender) {
        if (firstRender) {
            Console.WriteLine("First Render Complete");
        }
    }
}
```

3.7 Building Dynamic Components

Dynamic components allow you to render different components at runtime based on user actions or data. Blazor provides several ways to achieve dynamic component rendering, including conditional logic and dynamic component loading.

Subtopics to Cover:

- **Conditional Rendering**: Rendering different UI elements based on the state of your application using if and else statements.
- **Dynamically Adding Components**: Using the DynamicComponent class to load components dynamically at runtime.
- **Building a Tabbed Interface**: Example of creating a tabbed component interface where each tab loads a different child component.

Example for Dynamic Component Loading:

```razor
Copy code
@code {
    private Type ComponentToRender = typeof(FirstComponent);

    private void LoadSecondComponent() {
        ComponentToRender = typeof(SecondComponent);
    }
}
```

3.8 Interoperability with JavaScript

Even though Blazor Server allows you to avoid JavaScript for most tasks, there are scenarios where JavaScript interop is necessary. This section explores how to call JavaScript functions from C# and vice versa.

Subtopics to Cover:

- **Calling JavaScript Functions from C#**: Using IJSRuntime to invoke JavaScript functions from Razor components.
- **Invoking C# Methods from JavaScript**: Allowing JavaScript to call C# methods using the DotNetObjectReference.

- **Handling JavaScript Errors**: Strategies for error handling in JavaScript interop scenarios.

Example for JavaScript Interop:

```razor
Copy code
@inject IJSRuntime JS

<button @onclick="ShowAlert">Show Alert</button>

@code {
    private async Task ShowAlert() {
        await JS.InvokeVoidAsync("alert", "Hello from Blazor!");
    }
}
```

3.9 Managing Component State Across the Application

For complex applications, managing state between components is crucial. This section focuses on various strategies for state management in Blazor Server applications.

Subtopics to Cover:

- **Using Cascading Values and Parameters**: Passing data to child components without explicitly specifying it as a parameter.
- **Dependency Injection for State Management**: Leveraging services to manage shared state between multiple components.
- **Creating a State Container**: Implementing a state container pattern to manage state changes in a centralized place.

Example for Cascading Values:

```razor
Copy code
```

```
// MainLayout.razor
<CascadingValue Value="SharedData">
    @Body
</CascadingValue>

@code {
    private string SharedData = "This is a shared value";
}
```

3.10 Debugging and Troubleshooting Razor Components

Developing Razor components can sometimes involve issues related to data binding, event handling, or state management. This section provides practical debugging techniques and common troubleshooting tips.

Subtopics to Cover:

- **Using Visual Studio Debugger**: Setting breakpoints and stepping through Razor component code.
- **Inspecting HTML and SignalR Connections**: Using browser developer tools to inspect HTML elements and monitor the SignalR connection.
- **Common Errors and Solutions**: A list of common issues developers encounter in Razor components and how to resolve them.

Example of Debugging Tips:

- Set breakpoints in your Razor component by adding a C# method and stepping into it using the Visual Studio debugger.
- Use the **Blazor DevTools** browser extension to inspect the component hierarchy and analyze component rendering issues.

Conclusion

At the end of Chapter 3, readers will have a deep understanding of how Razor components work and how to build interactive and reusable components for Blazor Server applications. This knowledge forms the foundation for more advanced topics such as state management, API integration, and dynamic rendering, which will be covered in future chapters.

Chapter 4: Working with Data and APIs in Blazor Server

4.1 Introduction to Data Management in Blazor Server

Data is at the core of every interactive web application. Whether you're working with user forms, displaying dynamic content, or connecting to a database, understanding how to handle and manage data is crucial for building effective applications. This chapter introduces data management and interactions with APIs in Blazor Server, focusing on fetching, updating, and displaying data.

4.2 Connecting Blazor Server to a Data Source

To build a dynamic and data-driven application, you need to connect your Blazor Server app to a database. This section discusses the essential steps to establish a connection using Entity Framework Core.

Subtopics to Cover:

- **Introduction to Entity Framework Core**: Overview of Entity Framework Core (EF Core) as the primary ORM (Object-Relational Mapping) tool in Blazor Server projects.
- **Creating a Data Context**: How to define and set up a DbContext class for your application's database connection.
- **Configuring Database Migrations**: Using migrations to create and update database schemas automatically.

- **Dependency Injection for Data Contexts**: Registering your DbContext in the ASP.NET Core Dependency Injection (DI) container.

Content Example:

- **Creating a Data Context Class**:

```csharp
Copy code
public class AppDbContext : DbContext
{
    public AppDbContext
(DbContextOptions<AppDbContext> options)
: base(options)
    {
    }

    public DbSet<Product> Products { get; set; }
}
```

- **Configuring Services in Startup.cs**:

```csharp
Copy code
services.AddDbContext<AppDbContext>(options =>
    options.UseSqlServer(Configuration.
GetConnectionString("DefaultConnection")));
```

4.3 CRUD Operations with Entity Framework Core

CRUD (Create, Read, Update, Delete) operations are fundamental to working with data in any application. In Blazor Server, EF Core makes these operations straightforward. This section covers each operation in detail and provides hands-on examples.

Subtopics to Cover:

- **Creating Records**: Inserting new records into the database.
- **Reading and Displaying Data**: Querying and displaying data in Razor components using LINQ.
- **Updating Existing Records**: Modifying existing data and persisting changes to the database.
- **Deleting Records**: Removing records from the database.
- **Handling Errors and Validations**: Error handling and validation logic in CRUD operations.

Content Example:

- **Creating a Record**:

```csharp
Copy code
private async Task AddProduct()
{
    var newProduct = new Product
{ Name = "New Product", Price = 19.99M };
    _dbContext.Products.Add(newProduct);
    await _dbContext.SaveChangesAsync();
}
```

4.4 Fetching Data with HTTP Client in Blazor Server

Blazor Server supports making HTTP requests to external APIs using HttpClient. This section explains how to perform GET, POST, PUT, and DELETE requests to interact with RESTful APIs.

Subtopics to Cover:

- **Setting Up HttpClient in Blazor Server**: How to inject and configure the HttpClient service in Blazor Server.
- **Making GET Requests to Fetch Data**: Retrieving data from a REST

API and displaying it in a component.

- **Making POST Requests to Send Data**: Sending data to an external API.
- **Handling PUT and DELETE Requests**: Updating and deleting resources via external APIs.
- **Handling Asynchronous Operations**: Best practices for working with async/await and managing tasks in Blazor.

Content Example:

- **GET Request Example**:

```razor
Copy code
@inject HttpClient Http

<ul>
    @foreach (var item in products)
    {
        <li>@item.Name - @item.Price</li>
    }
</ul>

@code {
    private List<Product> products;

    protected override async Task OnInitializedAsync()
    {
        products = await Http.
GetFromJsonAsync<List<Product>>
("https://api.example.com/products");
    }
}
```

4.5 Form Handling and User Input Management

Handling user input effectively is critical in building web applications.

This section discusses how to build forms using the Blazor <EditForm> component, how to use input validation, and how to bind form data to model properties.

Subtopics to Cover:

- **Creating Forms with <EditForm>**: Basic structure of an <EditForm> component in Blazor.
- **Using Data Annotations for Validation**: Applying data annotations for input validation.
- **Custom Validations**: Implementing custom validation logic using validation attributes.
- **Handling Form Submissions**: Managing the form submission process and persisting data to a database.

Content Example:

- **Creating a Simple Form**:

```razor
Copy code
<EditForm Model="@product" OnValidSubmit="HandleSubmit">
    <DataAnnotationsValidator />
    <ValidationSummary />

    <label for="name">Product Name:</label>
    <InputText id="name" @bind-Value="product.Name" />
    <ValidationMessage For="@(() => product.Name)" />

    <label for="price">Price:</label>
    <InputNumber id="price" @bind-Value="product.Price" />
    <ValidationMessage For="@(() => product.Price)" />

    <button type="submit">Submit</button>
</EditForm>
```

```
@code {
    private Product product = new Product();

    private void HandleSubmit()
    {
        // Save the product to the database.
    }
}
```

4.6 Handling Asynchronous Data Operations

In Blazor Server, asynchronous programming is crucial for making non-blocking API calls and performing data operations without freezing the user interface. This section delves into the async/await pattern and its use in Blazor.

Subtopics to Cover:

- **Understanding Asynchronous Programming**: Overview of the async/await pattern and how it applies to Blazor Server.
- **Making Asynchronous API Calls**: Performing asynchronous HTTP requests using HttpClient.
- **Handling Long-Running Operations**: Best practices for handling long-running tasks, including loading indicators and progress notifications.
- **Optimizing Asynchronous Code**: Tips for optimizing async methods and avoiding common pitfalls.

Content Example:

- **Asynchronous Method Example**:

```csharp
Copy code
private async Task LoadProductsAsync()
{
    products = await Http.
GetFromJsonAsync<List<Product>>
("https://api.example.com/products");
}
```

4.7 State Management and Data Caching

In Blazor Server, managing state and caching data efficiently is essential to create responsive and performant applications. This section discusses different approaches to managing component state and caching frequently accessed data.

Subtopics to Cover:

- **Using State Containers**: Implementing a state container pattern to manage shared state between components.
- **Caching Data in Memory**: Strategies for caching data in memory to reduce API calls and enhance performance.
- **Working with Session Storage**: Leveraging session storage for temporary data persistence in the client's browser.
- **Best Practices for State Management**: Guidelines for choosing the right state management strategy based on application requirements.

Content Example:

- **Implementing a Simple State Container**:

```csharp
Copy code
public class AppState
{
```

```
    public string CurrentUser { get; set; }
}
```

- Injecting it into components:

```razor
razor
Copy code
@inject AppState State
```

4.8 Working with Real-Time Data Using SignalR

SignalR is a library for adding real-time web functionality to your Blazor Server application. It allows server-side updates to be pushed to the client immediately, without the need for the client to request the update.

Subtopics to Cover:

- **Setting Up SignalR in Blazor Server**: Configuring SignalR in a Blazor Server application.
- **Creating a SignalR Hub**: Defining a SignalR hub to handle real-time connections.
- **Handling Real-Time Data Updates**: Implementing real-time notifications and data updates in Blazor components.
- **Common Use Cases for SignalR**: Examples of where SignalR fits best, such as chat applications, real-time dashboards, and collaborative tools.

Content Example:

- **Defining a SignalR Hub**:

```csharp
csharp
Copy code
public class ChatHub : Hub
{
    public async Task SendMessage
(string user, string message)
    {
        await Clients.All.SendAsync(
"ReceiveMessage", user, message);
    }
}
```

4.9 Managing Data with RESTful APIs

RESTful APIs are widely used to interact with back-end services. In this section, we discuss the principles of REST and demonstrate how to design and consume RESTful APIs in Blazor Server applications.

Subtopics to Cover:

- **Understanding REST Principles**: Overview of REST principles and best practices for building RESTful APIs.
- **Consuming RESTful APIs in Blazor Server**: Example of consuming RESTful APIs using HttpClient and handling responses.
- **Sending Data to APIs**: How to structure POST and PUT requests to update data on the server.
- **Paginating and Filtering API Data**: Implementing pagination and filters to efficiently handle large datasets.

Content Example:

- **Pagination Example**:

```razor
razor
Copy code
```

```
<button @onclick="LoadNextPage">Next</button>

@code {
    private int currentPage = 1;

    private async Task LoadNextPage()
    {
        currentPage++;
        products = await Http.
GetFromJsonAsync<List<Product>>
($"https://api.example.
com/products?page={currentPage}");
    }
}
```

4.10 Handling Errors and Exceptions in Data Operations

Error handling is a crucial part of working with data and APIs. This section covers how to handle exceptions gracefully and provide meaningful feedback to users.

Subtopics to Cover:

- **Handling HTTP Errors**: Detecting and managing HTTP errors when making API calls.
- **Displaying Error Messages to Users**: Best practices for displaying error messages and handling validation errors in forms.
- **Logging Errors for Debugging**: Using ASP.NET Core's logging infrastructure to log exceptions and trace issues.

Content Example:

- **Error Handling Example**:

```csharp
csharp
Copy code
try
{
    products = await Http.
GetFromJsonAsync<List<Product>>
("https://api.example.com/products");
}
catch (HttpRequestException ex)
{
    // Handle error and display a message to the user.
}
```

Conclusion

At the end of Chapter 4, readers should have a comprehensive understanding of how to work with data and APIs in Blazor Server. They will know how to perform CRUD operations with Entity Framework Core, consume RESTful APIs using HttpClient, handle form data and user input, and manage application state effectively. With this knowledge, they will be well-equipped to build data-driven and interactive applications using Blazor Server.

Chapter 5: Mastering Form Handling and Validation in Blazor Server

5.1 Introduction to Form Handling in Blazor Server

Forms are a fundamental part of any web application, allowing users to input data and interact with the application. In Blazor Server, handling forms involves binding user input to model properties, validating that input, and managing the submission process. This chapter will explore how to create forms, handle user input, and implement validation using Blazor's built-in capabilities.

5.2 Creating Basic Forms with Blazor

The <EditForm> component in Blazor Server provides a straightforward way to create forms. This section discusses the structure of a basic form and how to bind it to a model.

Subtopics to Cover:

- **Using <EditForm>**: Introduction to the <EditForm> component and its purpose in Blazor.

- **Binding Form Fields to Model Properties**: How to bind input fields to properties of a model using the @bind directive.

- **Basic Input Components**: Overview of common input components available in Blazor, such as <InputText>, <InputNumber>, <InputDate>, and others.

Content Example:

- **Creating a Simple Form**:

```razor
Copy code
<EditForm Model="@product" OnValidSubmit="HandleValidSubmit">
    <DataAnnotationsValidator />
    <ValidationSummary />

    <label for="name">Product Name:</label>
    <InputText id="name" @bind-Value="product.Name" />
    <ValidationMessage For="@(() => product.Name)" />

    <label for="price">Price:</label>
    <InputNumber id="price" @bind-Value="product.Price" />
    <ValidationMessage For="@(() => product.Price)" />

    <button type="submit">Submit</button>
</EditForm>

@code {
    private Product product = new Product();

    private void HandleValidSubmit()
    {
        // Save the product to the database or perform other
        actions.
    }
}
```

5.3 Data Binding and Input Handling

Understanding data binding is crucial for effectively managing user input in forms. This section explores different types of binding available in Blazor.

Subtopics to Cover:

- **One-Way vs. Two-Way Data Binding**: Explanation of the difference between one-way and two-way data binding, including use cases for each.

- **Using @bind for Two-Way Binding**: Demonstration of how to use the @bind directive to establish two-way data binding for input fields.
- **Handling Input Events**: Techniques for capturing user input through events like oninput, onchange, and onclick.

Content Example:

- **Two-Way Binding Example**:

```razor
Copy code
<input type="text" @bind="product.Name" />
<p>You entered: @product.Name</p>
```

5.4 Validating User Input

Validating user input is essential to ensure data integrity and provide a good user experience. Blazor supports data validation through data annotations and custom validation logic.

Subtopics to Cover:

- **Using Data Annotations**: Introduction to data annotations such as [Required], [StringLength], and [Range] for validating model properties.
- **Displaying Validation Messages**: How to use <ValidationMessage> to display validation errors to users.
- **Custom Validation Attributes**: Creating custom validation attributes for more complex validation scenarios.

Content Example:

- **Data Annotation Example**:

```csharp
csharp
Copy code
public class Product
{
    [Required(ErrorMessage = "Product name is required.")]
    public string Name { get; set; }

    [Range(0.01, 1000, ErrorMessage = "Price must be between
    $0.01 and $1000.")]
    public decimal Price { get; set; }
}
```

5.5 Advanced Form Handling Techniques

In more complex scenarios, you may need to implement advanced form handling techniques to enhance user experience and manage more sophisticated use cases.

Subtopics to Cover:

- **Conditional Form Fields**: Implementing logic to show or hide fields based on user input or application state.
- **Dynamic Forms**: Building forms that adapt based on data or user choices, such as a multi-step form.
- **Using JavaScript for Enhanced User Experience**: Leveraging JavaScript interop for functionalities that go beyond Blazor's capabilities, such as rich text editors or file uploads.

Content Example:

- **Conditional Field Example**:

```razor
razor
Copy code
```

```
<InputCheckbox @bind="isDiscounted" />
@if (isDiscounted)
{
    <InputNumber id="discount" @bind-Value="product.Discount" />
}
```

5.6 Managing Form Submission and State

Handling form submissions involves managing state, processing data, and providing feedback to users. This section covers best practices for managing form submissions effectively.

Subtopics to Cover:

- **Managing Loading States**: How to provide feedback to users during form submission using loading indicators.
- **Handling Successful Submissions**: Best practices for showing success messages or redirecting users after a successful submission.
- **Error Handling on Submission**: Strategies for handling errors during submission, including API call failures or validation errors.

Content Example:

- **Handling Submission Example**:

```
razor
Copy code
private bool isSubmitting = false;

private async Task HandleValidSubmit()
{
    isSubmitting = true;
    await SaveProductAsync(product);
    isSubmitting = false;
    // Show success message
```

```
}
```

5.7 Using Blazor's Validation Summary and Validation Messages

Blazor provides built-in components for displaying validation summaries and specific validation messages. This section explains how to use these components effectively.

Subtopics to Cover:

- **Validation Summary**: Overview of how to use <ValidationSummary> to display a summary of all validation errors in the form.
- **Field-Specific Validation Messages**: Using <ValidationMessage> to show errors next to specific input fields.
- **Styling Validation Messages**: Techniques for styling validation messages for better user experience.

Content Example:

- **Using Validation Summary**:

```razor
Copy code
<ValidationSummary />
```

5.8 Form Data Management and State Persistence

Managing form data effectively across sessions can significantly enhance user experience. This section discusses how to persist form data and manage state.

Subtopics to Cover:

- **Session State vs. Local State**: Overview of the differences and when to use session state versus local component state.
- **Persisting State with Local Storage**: How to use browser local storage

to persist form data between sessions.

- **Retrieving Data on Component Initialization**: Loading persisted data back into the form when the component initializes.

Content Example:

- **Using Local Storage Example**:

```csharp
Copy code
private async Task SaveToLocalStorage()
{
    await JS.InvokeVoidAsync("localStorage.setItem",
    "productData", JsonSerializer.Serialize(product));
}

private async Task LoadFromLocalStorage()
{
    var data = await
    JS.InvokeAsync<string>("localStorage.getItem", "productData");
    if (!string.IsNullOrEmpty(data))
    {
        product = JsonSerializer.Deserialize<Product>(data);
    }
}
```

5.9 Best Practices for Building Forms in Blazor

To create effective forms in Blazor, following best practices can help improve usability and maintainability. This section outlines key strategies and patterns for building forms.

Subtopics to Cover:

- **Component Reusability**: Creating reusable form components for common input patterns, reducing redundancy in your codebase.
- **Consistent Validation Logic**: Implementing consistent validation

strategies across all forms to ensure a uniform user experience.

- **Accessibility Considerations**: Best practices for making forms accessible to all users, including screen readers and keyboard navigation.

Content Example:

- **Reusable Component Example**:

```razor
Copy code
// InputTextWithLabel.razor
<label for="@Id">@Label</label>
<InputText id="@Id" @bind-Value="@Value" />

@code {
    [Parameter] public string Label { get; set; }
    [Parameter] public string Id { get; set; }
    [Parameter] public string Value { get; set; }
}
```

5.10 Common Challenges and Troubleshooting Form Issues

Developing forms can lead to various challenges. This section provides troubleshooting tips for common form-related issues and how to overcome them.

Subtopics to Cover:

- **Common Validation Errors**: Identifying and resolving common validation errors users encounter.
- **Debugging Form Submission Issues**: Techniques for diagnosing issues related to form submission and data processing.
- **Handling API Errors Gracefully**: Strategies for managing errors returned from API calls during form submission.

Content Example:

- **Debugging Tips**:
- Use browser developer tools to inspect network requests and responses.
- Add logging statements in your C# code to trace the flow of data and identify issues.

Conclusion

At the end of Chapter 5, readers will have a comprehensive understanding of form handling and validation in Blazor Server. They will be equipped with the skills to create interactive, user-friendly forms that effectively manage data and validate user input. This knowledge is crucial for building responsive applications that meet users' needs.

Chapter 6: Managing State in Blazor Server Applications

6.1 Introduction to State Management in Blazor

State management is a critical aspect of web applications, particularly for applications that require dynamic content updates based on user interactions. In Blazor Server, state refers to any data that is stored during the user session and may be modified throughout the application lifecycle. This chapter explores how to effectively manage state in Blazor Server applications, focusing on different techniques and patterns to maintain a responsive user experience.

6.2 Understanding Different Types of State

Before delving into state management strategies, it's essential to understand the different types of state in a Blazor application.

Subtopics to Cover:

- **Component State**: This is local to a component and exists for the lifespan of that component. When the component is disposed, its state is lost.
- **Session State**: Data that persists across different components but is limited to a user's session.
- **Application State**: Data that is shared across all users and sessions. It typically resides on the server and can be accessed by multiple users.

Content Example:

- **Example of Component State:**

```razor
Copy code
@code {
    private int count = 0;

    private void IncrementCount()
    {
        count++;
    }
}
```

6.3 Using Component State Effectively

Component state management is often the simplest form of state management in Blazor. Components can hold state data that is relevant to their functionality. However, managing state effectively is essential to prevent unwanted behavior and ensure a smooth user experience.

Subtopics to Cover:

- **Local State Management**: Best practices for managing state that is specific to a component.
- **Lifecycle Methods**: Utilizing lifecycle methods (OnInitialized, OnParametersSet, OnAfterRender) to manage component state effectively.
- **Performance Considerations**: How to manage state efficiently to minimize performance bottlenecks.

Content Example:

- **Managing State in Lifecycle Methods:**

```razor
Copy code
@code {
    private string message;

    protected override void OnInitialized()
    {
        message = "Hello, welcome!";
    }
}
```

6.4 Implementing State Containers for Shared State

When managing state across multiple components, state containers provide a robust solution. A state container is a class that holds shared state and notifies components of state changes.

Subtopics to Cover:

- **Creating a State Container Class**: Defining a class that holds shared data and provides methods to modify it.
- **Using Dependency Injection**: Registering the state container with the service container for dependency injection.
- **Notifying Components of State Changes**: Using events to notify components when state changes occur.

Content Example:

- **State Container Example**:

```csharp
Copy code
public class AppState
{
    public string UserName { get; set; }
```

```
public event Action OnChange;

public void SetUserName(string userName)
{
    UserName = userName;
    NotifyStateChanged();
}

private void NotifyStateChanged() => OnChange?.Invoke();
}
```

- **Registering in Startup.cs**:

```
csharp
Copy code
services.AddScoped<AppState>();
```

6.5 Managing Session State in Blazor Server

Session state allows you to persist data across different components within a user's session. This is particularly useful for scenarios where you want to maintain user preferences or cart data across multiple pages.

Subtopics to Cover:

- **Using ProtectedSessionStorage**: How to store and retrieve data using Blazor's ProtectedSessionStorage service.
- **Persisting Data Across Sessions**: Strategies for keeping data accessible throughout a user's interaction with the application.
- **Best Practices for Session Management**: How to handle session expiration and clean up session data effectively.

Content Example:

- **Storing Data in Session Storage**:

```razor
Copy code
@inject ProtectedSessionStorage sessionStorage

private async Task SaveUserName(string userName)
{
    await sessionStorage.SetAsync("UserName", userName);
}

private async Task LoadUserName()
{
    var result = await
    sessionStorage.GetAsync<string>("UserName");
    if (result.Success)
    {
        // Use the stored UserName
    }
}
```

6.6 Managing Application State in Blazor

Application state is shared across all users and sessions. In Blazor Server, this state is typically stored on the server and can be accessed globally. Managing application state requires a different approach compared to component or session state.

Subtopics to Cover:

- **Global Services for Application State**: Creating services that maintain application-wide state.
- **Handling Concurrency**: Strategies for managing data access when multiple users interact with the same application state.
- **Data Caching**: Implementing caching strategies to optimize performance and reduce server load.

Content Example:

- **Global Service Example**:

```csharp
Copy code
public class ProductService
{
    private readonly List<Product> products = new List<Product>();

    public IEnumerable<Product> GetProducts() => products;

    public void AddProduct(Product product) =>
    products.Add(product);
}
```

6.7 State Management with Blazor's Component Parameters

Passing data between components using parameters is a common state management technique. This section discusses how to effectively use component parameters to share state between parent and child components.

Subtopics to Cover:

- **Defining Component Parameters**: Using the [Parameter] attribute to define properties that can receive data.
- **Two-Way Binding with Parameters**: Implementing two-way data binding to allow parent components to update child component parameters.
- **Handling Changes in Parameters**: Reacting to changes in parameter values and updating component state accordingly.

Content Example:

- **Two-Way Binding Example**:

```razor
Copy code
// ParentComponent.razor
<ChildComponent @bind-Value="parentValue" />

@code {
    private string parentValue = "Initial Value";
}
```

6.8 State Management Patterns in Blazor

Various design patterns can be employed for state management in Blazor applications. This section discusses some common patterns and their appropriate use cases.

Subtopics to Cover:

- **Observer Pattern**: Implementing the observer pattern for managing state updates and notifications.
- **Singleton Pattern**: Using the singleton pattern for services that maintain global state throughout the application's lifetime.
- **Flux and Redux Patterns**: An introduction to Flux and Redux-like patterns for managing state in complex applications.

Content Example:

- **Implementing the Observer Pattern**:

```csharp
Copy code
public class StateObserver
{
    private readonly List<IObserver> observers = new
    List<IObserver>();
```

```
public void Attach(IObserver observer) =>
observers.Add(observer);
public void Notify() => observers.ForEach(o => o.Update());
}
```

6.9 Debugging State Management Issues

Debugging state-related issues can be challenging. This section provides practical strategies for diagnosing and fixing common state management problems in Blazor applications.

Subtopics to Cover:

- **Common State Management Issues**: Identifying and troubleshooting issues related to state synchronization and unexpected behavior.
- **Using Debugging Tools**: Utilizing built-in debugging tools and techniques in Visual Studio to track down state-related bugs.
- **Logging State Changes**: Implementing logging to monitor state changes and identify potential problems.

Content Example:

- **Logging Example**:

```csharp
Copy code
private void NotifyStateChanged()
{
    _logger.LogInformation("State changed to: {State}",
    currentState);
    OnChange?.Invoke();
}
```

6.10 Best Practices for State Management in Blazor Server

To ensure effective state management in your Blazor applications, it's essential to follow best practices. This section outlines key recommendations for managing state effectively.

Subtopics to Cover:

- **Keep State Local Where Possible**: Prefer component state over global state to reduce complexity.
- **Leverage Dependency Injection**: Use DI to manage shared state containers and services effectively.
- **Minimize State Size**: Keep state as small as possible to improve performance and reduce memory usage.
- **Handle Cleanup**: Ensure proper cleanup of state data when it is no longer needed to prevent memory leaks.

Content Example:

- **Best Practices Summary**:
- Use component state for transient data.
- Implement cleanup logic in Dispose methods for state containers.
- Regularly review and refactor state management logic for clarity and efficiency.

Conclusion

By the end of Chapter 6, readers will have a comprehensive understanding of state management in Blazor Server applications. They will learn how to effectively manage component state, session state, and application state, as well as apply best practices for ensuring a smooth user experience. With this knowledge, they will be well-prepared to build responsive and dynamic applications that handle user interactions seamlessly.

Chapter 7: Implementing Authentication and Authorization in Blazor Server

7.1 Introduction to Authentication and Authorization

Authentication and authorization are critical aspects of web applications that deal with user identity and access control. In a Blazor Server application, these processes ensure that only authorized users can access specific resources and perform certain actions.

- **Authentication** verifies who a user is. It involves processes that confirm the identity of a user based on credentials such as usernames and passwords.
- **Authorization** determines what an authenticated user is allowed to do. This involves setting permissions and roles that dictate user access to various parts of the application.

This chapter will guide you through implementing authentication and authorization in Blazor Server applications using ASP.NET Core Identity and role-based access control.

7.2 Setting Up Authentication in Blazor Server

To implement authentication in a Blazor Server application, you first need to configure the authentication services. This section covers how to set up authentication using ASP.NET Core Identity.

Subtopics to Cover:

- **Installing Required Packages**: Using NuGet to install the necessary packages for ASP.NET Core Identity.
- **Configuring Identity Services**: Setting up Identity in the Startup.cs file, including configuring the identity options.
- **Setting Up Database Context**: Configuring the database context for storing user information and managing authentication.

Content Example:

1. **Install ASP.NET Core Identity**: Open the NuGet Package Manager Console and run:

```bash
Copy code
Install-Package Microsoft.AspNetCore.
Identity.EntityFrameworkCore
Install-Package Microsoft.AspNetCore.
Authentication.Cookies
```

1. **Configure Identity in Startup.cs**:

```csharp
Copy code
public void ConfigureServices(IServiceCollection services)
{
    services.AddDbContext<ApplicationDbContext>(options =>
        options.UseSqlServer(Configuration.
GetConnectionString("DefaultConnection")));

    services.AddIdentity<IdentityUser, IdentityRole>()
```

```
    .AddEntityFrameworkStores<ApplicationDbContext>()
    .AddDefaultTokenProviders();

services.Configure<IdentityOptions>(options =>
{
    options.Password.RequireDigit = true;
    options.Password.RequiredLength = 6;
    options.Password.RequireNonAlphanumeric = false;
    options.Password.RequireUppercase = true;
    options.Password.RequireLowercase = true;
});

services.AddRazorPages();
services.AddServerSideBlazor();
}
```

7.3 Implementing User Registration and Login

Once authentication is set up, you can implement user registration and login functionalities. This section will guide you through creating the necessary UI components and backend logic.

Subtopics to Cover:

- **Creating the Registration Component**: Building a Blazor component for user registration that collects user details.
- **Implementing Registration Logic**: Writing the backend logic to create a new user account using ASP.NET Core Identity.
- **Creating the Login Component**: Building a component for user login, including input fields for credentials.

Content Example:

1. **Registration Component**:

```razor
Copy code
@page "/register"
@inject UserManager<IdentityUser> UserManager
@inject NavigationManager Navigation

<EditForm Model="@user" OnValidSubmit="RegisterUser">
    <DataAnnotationsValidator />
    <ValidationSummary />

    <InputText id="username" @bind-Value="user.UserName"
    placeholder="Username" />
    <InputText id="email" @bind-Value="user.Email"
    placeholder="Email" />
    <InputText id="password" type=
"password" @bind-Value="password"
placeholder="Password" />
    <InputText id="confirmPassword" type="password"
    @bind-Value="confirmPassword" placeholder="Confirm Password"
    />

    <button type="submit">Register</button>
</EditForm>

@code {
    private IdentityUser user = new IdentityUser();
    private string password;
    private string confirmPassword;

    private async Task RegisterUser()
    {
        if (password != confirmPassword)
        {
            // Show error message
            return;
        }

        var result = await UserManager.
CreateAsync(user, password);
        if (result.Succeeded)
```

```
        {
            Navigation.NavigateTo("/login");
        }
    }
}
```

1. **Login Component**:

```razor
razor
Copy code
@page "/login"
@inject SignInManager<IdentityUser> SignInManager
@inject NavigationManager Navigation

<EditForm Model="@loginModel" OnValidSubmit="LoginUser">
    <DataAnnotationsValidator />
    <ValidationSummary />

    <InputText id="username" @bind-
Value="loginModel.UserName" placeholder="Username" />
    <InputText id="password" type="password"
    @bind-Value="loginModel.Password" placeholder="Password" />

    <button type="submit">Login</button>
</EditForm>

@code {
    private LoginModel loginModel = new LoginModel();

    private async Task LoginUser()
    {
        var result = await
        SignInManager.PasswordSignInAsync(loginModel.UserName,
        loginModel.Password, isPersistent:
    false, lockoutOnFailure: false);
        if (result.Succeeded)
```

```
        {
            Navigation.NavigateTo("/");
        }
        else
        {
            // Show error message
        }
    }

    public class LoginModel
    {
        public string UserName { get; set; }
        public string Password { get; set; }
    }
}
```

7.4 Implementing Logout Functionality

Once users can log in, providing a way for them to log out is crucial for security and user experience. This section explains how to implement logout functionality in a Blazor Server application.

Subtopics to Cover:

- **Creating a Logout Component**: Building a simple component or button to handle user logout.
- **Implementing Logout Logic**: Writing the backend logic to sign out the user.

Content Example:

- **Logout Logic**:

```razor
Copy code
@page "/logout"
@inject SignInManager<IdentityUser> SignInManager
```

```
@inject NavigationManager Navigation

@code {
    protected override async Task OnInitializedAsync()
    {
        await SignInManager.SignOutAsync();
        Navigation.NavigateTo("/");
    }
}
```

7.5 Role-Based Authorization

Role-based authorization allows you to restrict access to certain parts of your application based on user roles. This section will guide you through implementing role-based access control.

Subtopics to Cover:

- **Defining User Roles**: How to create roles in your application using ASP.NET Core Identity.
- **Assigning Roles to Users**: Writing the logic to assign roles to users during registration or through an admin interface.
- **Using [Authorize] Attribute**: Implementing the [Authorize] attribute to protect specific pages or components based on user roles.

Content Example:

1. **Creating and Assigning Roles**:

```
csharp
Copy code
public async Task InitializeRoles(RoleManager<IdentityRole>
roleManager)
{
    string[] roleNames = { "Admin", "User" };
```

```
foreach (var roleName in roleNames)
{
    if (!await roleManager.RoleExistsAsync(roleName))
    {
        await roleManager.CreateAsync(new
        IdentityRole(roleName));
    }
}

var user = await
UserManager.FindByEmailAsync("admin@example.com");
await UserManager.AddToRoleAsync(user, "Admin");
}
```

1. **Using the [Authorize] Attribute**:

```razor
Copy code
@page "/admin"
@attribute [Authorize(Roles = "Admin")]

<h3>Admin Page</h3>
```

7.6 Claims-Based Authorization

Claims-based authorization allows for more granular control over user access by evaluating specific user claims. This section discusses how to implement claims-based authorization in your Blazor Server application.

Subtopics to Cover:

- **Understanding Claims**: What claims are and how they differ from roles.
- **Adding Claims to Users**: How to add claims to users during registration or through an admin interface.
- **Using Claims in Authorization**: Implementing logic to check for

specific claims in your application.

Content Example:

1. **Adding Claims to Users**:

```csharp
Copy code
await UserManager.AddClaimAsync(user, new Claim("CanEdit",
"true"));
```

1. **Using Claims for Authorization**:

```razor
Copy code
@page "/editor"
@attribute [Authorize(Policy = "CanEditPolicy")]

<h3>Editor Page</h3>
```

7.7 Customizing Authorization Policies

Custom authorization policies provide a powerful way to enforce complex security requirements. This section explains how to define and implement custom authorization policies in your Blazor Server application.

Subtopics to Cover:

- **Defining Authorization Policies**: How to create custom policies in Startup.cs.
- **Implementing Policy Requirements**: Writing classes that implement the IAuthorizationRequirement interface.
- **Using Policies in Components**: Applying custom policies to protect pages or components.

Content Example:

1. Defining a Custom Policy:

```csharp
Copy code
services.AddAuthorization(options =>
{
    options.AddPolicy("CanEditPolicy", policy =>
        policy.RequireClaim("CanEdit", "true"));
});
```

1. Using Custom Policies:

```razor
Copy code
@page "/restricted"
@attribute [Authorize(Policy = "CanEditPolicy")]

<h3>Restricted Page</h3>
```

7.8 Authentication State in Blazor

Blazor Server provides built-in support for managing authentication state, allowing you to access user information easily. This section covers how to work with the authentication state in your components.

Subtopics to Cover:

- **Using AuthenticationStateProvider**: How to inject and use AuthenticationStateProvider to get information about the authenticated user.
- **Displaying User Information**: Rendering user-specific information based on the authentication state.
- **Managing User Session State**: Techniques for handling user session

state effectively.

Content Example:

- **Accessing Authentication State**:

```razor
Copy code
@inject AuthenticationStateProvider AuthenticationStateProvider

@code {
    private async Task GetUser()
    {
        var authState = await
        AuthenticationStateProvider.GetAuthenticationStateAsync();
        var user = authState.User;

        if (user.Identity.IsAuthenticated)
        {
            // User is authenticated
        }
    }
}
```

7.9 Securing API Calls with Authentication

When building Blazor Server applications, it is essential to ensure that API calls are secure. This section discusses how to authenticate API requests and protect sensitive data.

Subtopics to Cover:

- **Using JWT Tokens for API Security**: Overview of JSON Web Tokens (JWT) and how to use them for securing API endpoints.
- **Passing Tokens in API Requests**: How to include authentication tokens in HTTP requests from Blazor components.
- **Validating Tokens on the Server**: Implementing token validation in

your API to ensure secure access.

Content Example:

1. Generating JWT Tokens:

```csharp
Copy code
public string GenerateJwtToken(IdentityUser user)
{
    var claims = new[]
    {
        new Claim(JwtRegisteredClaimNames.Sub, user.UserName),
        new Claim(JwtRegisteredClaimNames.Jti,
        Guid.NewGuid().ToString())
    };

    var key = new SymmetricSecurityKey(Encoding.UTF8.
GetBytes("YourSecretKey"));
    var creds = new SigningCredentials(key,
    SecurityAlgorithms.HmacSha256);

    var token = new JwtSecurityToken(
        issuer: "yourdomain.com",
        audience: "yourdomain.com",
        claims: claims,
        expires: DateTime.Now.AddMinutes(30),
        signingCredentials: creds);

    return new JwtSecurityTokenHandler().WriteToken(token);
}
```

1. Making Authenticated API Calls:

```csharp
Copy code
private async Task FetchData()
{
    var token = await GetJwtToken();
    Http.DefaultRequestHeaders.Authorization = new
    AuthenticationHeaderValue("Bearer", token);
    var data = await Http.
GetFromJsonAsync<List<YourDataType>>
("https://api.example.com/data");
}
```

7.10 Best Practices for Authentication and Authorization in Blazor

To ensure a secure and user-friendly authentication and authorization implementation, it is essential to follow best practices. This section outlines key recommendations for managing security effectively in Blazor applications.

Subtopics to Cover:

- **Regularly Update Packages**: Keep all NuGet packages and libraries updated to incorporate the latest security patches.
- **Use HTTPS**: Ensure all communication is secured using HTTPS to protect sensitive data.
- **Implement Strong Password Policies**: Use strong password policies and two-factor authentication (2FA) to enhance security.
- **Limit Data Exposure**: Implement role-based access control to limit what data users can access based on their roles.

Content Example:

- **Implementing 2FA:**

```csharp
csharp
Copy code
public async Task EnableTwoFactor
Authentication(IdentityUser user)
{
    var token = await UserManager.
GenerateTwoFactorTokenAsync(user, "Email");
    // Send token via email or SMS
}
```

Conclusion

By the end of Chapter 7, readers will have a comprehensive understanding of how to implement authentication and authorization in Blazor Server applications. They will learn how to set up user registration and login, manage user roles and claims, and secure API calls. With this knowledge, readers will be well-equipped to build secure, user-friendly applications that effectively manage user identities and access control.

Chapter 8: Working with Real-Time Data Using SignalR in Blazor Server

8.1 Introduction to SignalR

SignalR is an open-source library that simplifies the process of adding real-time web functionality to applications. It enables server-side code to push content to connected clients instantly, facilitating the development of applications that require high-frequency updates. Common use cases for SignalR include chat applications, live dashboards, real-time notifications, and collaborative tools.

In Blazor Server applications, SignalR is built-in, allowing developers to leverage its capabilities seamlessly. This chapter will guide you through integrating SignalR into your Blazor Server app, enabling real-time features that enhance user interactivity and engagement.

8.2 Setting Up SignalR in Blazor Server

To start using SignalR in a Blazor Server application, you need to configure your project to include the SignalR services. This section will walk you through the setup process.

Subtopics to Cover:

- **Installing SignalR Packages**: Using NuGet to install the necessary SignalR packages.
- **Configuring SignalR in Startup.cs**: Setting up SignalR services and

endpoints in your Blazor Server application.

- **Creating a SignalR Hub**: Understanding the role of hubs in SignalR and how to create one.

Content Example:

1. **Install SignalR Package**: Open the NuGet Package Manager Console and run:

```bash
Copy code
Install-Package Microsoft.AspNetCore.SignalR
```

1. **Configure SignalR in Startup.cs**:

```csharp
Copy code
public void ConfigureServices(IServiceCollection services)
{
    services.AddRazorPages();
    services.AddServerSideBlazor();
    services.AddSignalR(); // Register SignalR
}

public void Configure(IApplicationBuilder app,
IWebHostEnvironment env)
{
    app.UseRouting();

    app.UseEndpoints(endpoints =>
    {
        endpoints.MapBlazorHub();
        endpoints.MapHub<ChatHub>("/chathub"); // Map the hub
```

```
        endpoints.MapFallbackToPage("/_Host");
    });
}
```

1. **Creating a SignalR Hub**:

```csharp
Copy code
public class ChatHub : Hub
{
    public async Task SendMessage(string user, string message)
    {
        await Clients.All.SendAsync("ReceiveMessage", user,
        message);
    }
}
```

8.3 Understanding SignalR Hubs

Hubs are the core components of SignalR that facilitate communication between the client and the server. This section provides an in-depth look at SignalR hubs and their functionalities.

Subtopics to Cover:

- **What is a Hub?**: Definition and purpose of SignalR hubs.
- **Client-Server Communication**: Understanding how clients interact with hubs to send and receive messages.
- **Managing Connections**: Techniques for managing user connections and broadcasting messages.

Content Example:

- **Client-Server Interaction**:

```csharp
Copy code
public async Task SendMessage(string user, string message)
{
    await Clients.All.SendAsync("ReceiveMessage", user, message);
}
```

- **Managing Connections**:

```csharp
Copy code
public override async Task OnConnectedAsync()
{
    await Clients.All.SendAsync("UserConnected",
    Context.ConnectionId);
    await base.OnConnectedAsync();
}
```

8.4 Creating a Chat Application with SignalR

A practical way to understand SignalR is by building a simple chat application. This section will walk you through creating a real-time chat app using Blazor Server and SignalR.

Subtopics to Cover:

- **Creating the Chat Interface**: Designing the UI for the chat application.
- **Implementing the Chat Hub**: Setting up the SignalR hub to handle chat messages.
- **Connecting the Client to the Hub**: Writing the client-side logic to connect to the SignalR hub and handle messages.

Content Example:

1. **Creating the Chat Interface**:

```razor
Copy code
@page "/chat"

<h3>Chat Room</h3>
<input type="text" @bind="userName" placeholder="Your name" />
<textarea @bind="message" placeholder="Type a
message..."></textarea>
<button @onclick="SendMessage">Send</button>

<ul>
    @foreach (var msg in messages)
    {
        <li>@msg</li>
    }
</ul>

@code {
    private string userName;
    private string message;
    private List<string> messages = new List<string>();

    // SignalR connection logic will go here
}
```

1. **Implementing the Chat Hub**:

```csharp
Copy code
public class ChatHub : Hub
{
    public async Task SendMessage(string user, string message)
    {
```

```
        var msg = $"{user}: {message}";
        await Clients.All.SendAsync("ReceiveMessage", msg);
    }
}
```

1. **Connecting the Client to the Hub**:

```razor
razor
Copy code
@inject NavigationManager Navigation
@inject IHubContext<ChatHub> HubContext

protected override async Task OnInitializedAsync()
{
    var connection = new HubConnectionBuilder()
        .WithUrl(Navigation.ToAbsoluteUri("/chathub"))
        .Build();

    connection.On<string>("ReceiveMessage", (message) =>
    {
        messages.Add(message);
        InvokeAsync(StateHasChanged);
    });

    await connection.StartAsync();
}

private async Task SendMessage()
{
    await connection.InvokeAsync("SendMessage", userName,
    message);
    message = string.Empty; // Clear the input field
}
```

8.5 Managing User Connections in SignalR

Managing user connections is essential for personalizing the experience

82

and ensuring that messages reach the intended recipients. This section discusses how to manage connections and group users.

Subtopics to Cover:

- **Tracking Connected Users**: Keeping track of connected users and their connection IDs.
- **Creating User Groups**: How to group users for targeted message delivery.
- **Broadcasting Messages to Specific Groups**: Sending messages to specific groups rather than all connected clients.

Content Example:

1. **Tracking Connected Users**:

```csharp
Copy code
private static readonly HashSet<string> ConnectedUsers = new
HashSet<string>();

public override Task OnConnectedAsync()
{
    ConnectedUsers.Add(Context.ConnectionId);
    return base.OnConnectedAsync();
}
```

1. **Creating User Groups**:

```csharp
Copy code
public async Task JoinGroup(string groupName)
{
```

```
    await Groups.AddToGroupAsync(Context.ConnectionId, groupName);
}
```

1. **Broadcasting to Groups**:

```csharp
Copy code
public async Task SendMessageToGroup(string groupName, string
message)
{
    await Clients.Group(groupName).SendAsync("ReceiveMessage",
    message);
}
```

8.6 Real-Time Notifications and Updates

Incorporating real-time notifications enhances user experience by providing timely updates. This section will guide you through implementing notifications using SignalR.

Subtopics to Cover:

- **Sending Notifications from the Server**: How to send notifications to connected clients.
- **Displaying Notifications in the UI**: Creating UI elements to display notifications dynamically.
- **Managing Notification Settings**: Allowing users to customize notification preferences.

Content Example:

1. **Sending Notifications**:

```csharp
csharp
Copy code
public async Task NotifyUsers(string message)
{
    await Clients.All.SendAsync("ReceiveNotification", message);
}
```

1. Displaying Notifications in the UI:

```razor
razor
Copy code
<ul>
    @foreach (var notification in notifications)
    {
        <li>@notification</li>
    }
</ul>

@code {
    private List<string> notifications = new List<string>();

    protected override async Task OnInitializedAsync()
    {
        // Setup SignalR connection and handle notifications
        connection.On<string>("ReceiveNotification",
        (notification) =>
        {
            notifications.Add(notification);
            InvokeAsync(StateHasChanged);
        });
    }
}
```

8.7 Performance Considerations for SignalR in Blazor

While SignalR provides powerful real-time capabilities, managing performance is crucial to ensure a smooth user experience. This section discusses best practices for optimizing SignalR performance.

Subtopics to Cover:

- **Reducing Message Size**: Strategies for minimizing the size of messages sent over SignalR.
- **Throttling and Debouncing Events**: Techniques to limit the frequency of event calls to prevent overload.
- **Scaling SignalR Applications**: Options for scaling SignalR applications to handle a large number of concurrent connections.

Content Example:

1. **Reducing Message Size**:

- Consider sending only essential data in notifications and messages.

1. **Throttling and Debouncing Events**:

```csharp
Copy code
// Use throttling logic in the UI to limit the frequency of
sending messages
```

1. **Scaling SignalR Applications**:

- Discuss options such as Azure SignalR Service for scaling.

8.8 Security Best Practices with SignalR

Implementing security measures is crucial when using SignalR to prevent unauthorized access and attacks. This section provides guidelines for securing SignalR communications.

Subtopics to Cover:

- **Using HTTPS for SignalR Connections**: Ensuring all SignalR connections use HTTPS for secure data transmission.
- **Implementing Authentication**: Requiring authentication for SignalR hubs to ensure that only authorized users can connect.
- **Preventing Cross-Site Scripting (XSS)**: Best practices for preventing XSS attacks in SignalR applications.

Content Example:

1. **Enforcing HTTPS**:

```csharp
Copy code
app.UseHttpsRedirection();
```

1. **Securing Hubs with Authentication**:

```csharp
Copy code
[Authorize]
public class ChatHub : Hub
{
    // Hub methods
}
```

1. **Preventing XSS**:

- Sanitize user input and escape output to mitigate XSS vulnerabilities.

8.9 Debugging SignalR Applications

Debugging real-time applications can be challenging. This section covers techniques and tools for effectively debugging SignalR applications.

Subtopics to Cover:

- **Using Browser Developer Tools**: Leveraging the browser's developer tools to monitor WebSocket connections and SignalR communications.
- **Logging SignalR Events**: Implementing logging to capture important events and errors within SignalR.
- **Troubleshooting Common Issues**: Identifying and resolving common SignalR issues such as connection problems and authentication errors.

Content Example:

1. **Monitoring WebSocket Connections**:

- Use Chrome DevTools or similar tools to inspect WebSocket frames.

1. **Implementing Logging**:

```csharp
Copy code
// Example of logging SignalR events
```

8.10 Real-World Scenarios and Use Cases

Understanding how SignalR can be applied in real-world scenarios can help solidify concepts. This section discusses various use cases for SignalR in Blazor applications.

Subtopics to Cover:

- **Real-Time Chat Applications**: How SignalR can be used to build fully-featured chat applications.
- **Live Dashboards**: Creating dashboards that display real-time data and

updates.

- **Collaborative Applications**: Implementing features that allow multiple users to interact and collaborate in real-time.

Content Example:

1. **Building a Chat Application**:

- Describe the steps taken in a chat application and how SignalR enhances user interaction.

1. **Creating a Live Dashboard**:

```razor
Copy code
// Display real-time data updates in a dashboard format
```

Conclusion

By the end of Chapter 8, readers will have a comprehensive understanding of how to work with real-time data using SignalR in Blazor Server applications. They will learn how to set up SignalR, create chat applications, manage user connections, send notifications, and apply security best practices. With this knowledge, readers will be equipped to build interactive applications that enhance user engagement through real-time features.

Chapter 9: Implementing Routing and Navigation in Blazor Server Applications

9.1 Introduction to Routing in Blazor

Routing is a crucial aspect of any web application, as it determines how users navigate between different views and components. In Blazor Server, routing is built into the framework, allowing developers to define routes easily and manage navigation seamlessly.

- **What is Routing?**: Routing is the process of mapping a URL to a specific component, enabling users to navigate to different parts of the application through hyperlinks or programmatic navigation.
- **Blazor's Routing System**: Blazor uses a component-based routing system, which means that each route corresponds to a Razor component. This allows developers to create a clean, maintainable application structure.

This chapter will provide a thorough understanding of routing in Blazor Server, covering everything from basic routing to more advanced scenarios involving nested routes, route parameters, and programmatic navigation.

9.2 Basic Routing in Blazor Server

The simplest way to implement routing in a Blazor Server application is by defining routes using the @page directive in your Razor components. This section will introduce basic routing concepts and demonstrate how to create routes.

Subtopics to Cover:

- **The @page Directive**: Understanding the role of the @page directive in defining routes for Razor components.
- **Creating Your First Routes**: How to create and navigate between basic routes in your Blazor application.
- **The Router Component**: Overview of the <Router> component and its role in managing navigation.

Content Example:

1. **Using the @page Directive**:

```razor
Copy code
@page "/"

<h1>Welcome to the Blazor App!</h1>
```

1. **Creating Additional Routes**:

```razor
Copy code
@page "/about"

<h2>About Us</h2>
<p>This is the about page of our Blazor application.</p>
```

1. **Setting Up the Router**: In App.razor, set up the router:

```razor
Copy code
<Router AppAssembly="@typeof(Program).Assembly">
    <Found Context="routeData">
        <RouteView RouteData="@routeData"
        DefaultLayout="@typeof(MainLayout)" />
    </Found>
    <NotFound>
        <LayoutView Layout="@typeof(MainLayout)">
            <p>Sorry, there's nothing at this address.</p>
        </LayoutView>
    </NotFound>
</Router>
```

9.3 Navigating Between Routes

Blazor Server provides a few ways to navigate between different routes. This section will discuss how to implement navigation using links and programmatic navigation.

Subtopics to Cover:

- **Using <NavLink> for Navigation**: How to create navigation links that reflect the active route.
- **Programmatic Navigation with NavigationManager**: Implementing navigation in response to user actions or events using the Navigation-Manager service.
- **Handling Query Parameters in Navigation**: Passing and retrieving query parameters during navigation.

Content Example:

1. **Using <NavLink>:**

```razor
razor
Copy code
<NavLink href="/" class="nav-link">Home</NavLink>
<NavLink href="/about" class="nav-link">About</NavLink>
```

1. **Programmatic Navigation**:

```razor
razor
Copy code
@inject NavigationManager Navigation

private void GoToAbout()
{
    Navigation.NavigateTo("/about");
}
```

1. **Handling Query Parameters**:

```razor
razor
Copy code
@page "/search"
@code {
    [Parameter] public string Query { get; set; }

    protected override void OnParametersSet()
    {
        // Handle the search query
    }
}
```

9.4 Route Parameters and Optional Parameters

Blazor routing supports route parameters, allowing you to create dynamic routes that can accept values from the URL. This section will cover how to implement route parameters and make them optional.

Subtopics to Cover:

- **Defining Route Parameters**: How to define route parameters in the @page directive.
- **Retrieving Route Parameters**: Accessing route parameters in your components and using them in your application logic.
- **Making Parameters Optional**: Implementing optional parameters and handling cases when they are not provided.

Content Example:

1. **Defining Route Parameters**:

```razor
Copy code
@page "/user/{userId:int}"

@code {
    [Parameter] public int UserId { get; set; }

    protected override void OnParametersSet()
    {
        // Use the UserId parameter
    }
}
```

1. **Retrieving and Using Parameters**:

```razor
Copy code
<h3>User ID: @UserId</h3>
```

1. Making Parameters Optional:

```razor
Copy code
@page "/user/{userId:int?}"

@code {
    [Parameter] public int? UserId { get; set; }
}
```

9.5 Nested Routing in Blazor

Nested routing allows you to create a more complex navigation structure by defining routes within routes. This section discusses how to implement nested routing in Blazor Server applications.

Subtopics to Cover:

- **Creating Nested Routes**: How to define child routes within a parent component.
- **Using Layouts with Nested Routes**: Applying layouts to create a consistent UI across different nested routes.
- **Managing State in Nested Routes**: Techniques for managing state across parent and child components.

Content Example:

1. Creating Nested Routes:

```razor
razor
Copy code
@page "/products"
<RouteView RouteData="@routeData"
DefaultLayout="@typeof(MainLayout)" />
```

1. **Child Component Example**:

```razor
razor
Copy code
@page "/products/{productId:int}"

<h3>Product Details for Product ID: @productId</h3>
```

1. **Using Layouts**:

```razor
razor
Copy code
@layout MainLayout
```

9.6 Route Constraints and Custom Routes

Route constraints allow you to control how routes are matched based on the route parameters. This section will cover implementing route constraints and creating custom routes.

Subtopics to Cover:

- **Understanding Route Constraints**: Explanation of built-in route constraints and how they work.
- **Implementing Custom Route Constraints**: How to create custom route constraints for specific matching logic.

- **Using Route Constraints in Blazor**: Applying constraints to your route definitions for better control over routing.

Content Example:

1. **Built-in Route Constraints**:

```razor
Copy code
@page "/product/{id:int}"
```

1. **Custom Route Constraint Example**:

```csharp
Copy code
public class CustomRouteConstraint : IRouteConstraint
{
    public bool Match(HttpContext httpContext, string routeKey,
    RouteValueDictionary values, RouteDirection routeDirection)
    {
        // Custom matching logic
    }
}
```

1. **Applying Constraints in Routes**:

```razor
Copy code
@page "/custom/{value:customConstraint}"
```

9.7 Managing Navigation State

Maintaining navigation state is essential, especially in applications where users can navigate back and forth frequently. This section discusses strategies for managing navigation state in Blazor Server.

Subtopics to Cover:

- **Using NavigationManager for State Management**: How to use NavigationManager to track navigation history and state.
- **Implementing Back and Forward Navigation**: Techniques for managing browser navigation history in your application.
- **Persisting Navigation State Across Sessions**: Strategies for preserving navigation state when users leave and return to the application.

Content Example:

1. **Using NavigationManager**:

```csharp
Copy code
@inject NavigationManager Navigation
```

1. **Back and Forward Navigation**:

```razor
Copy code
<button @onclick="GoBack">Back</button>
<button @onclick="GoForward">Forward</button>

@code {
    private void GoBack() =>
```

```
Navigation.NavigateTo(Navigation.GetUriWithQueryString());
private void GoForward() =>
Navigation.NavigateTo(Navigation.GetUriWithQueryString());
}
```

1. **Persisting State**:

- Use local storage to save the current state when the user leaves the page.

9.8 Handling NotFound Pages

When users navigate to a route that doesn't exist, a proper user experience should provide a friendly error page. This section discusses how to implement NotFound handling in Blazor Server applications.

Subtopics to Cover:

- **Creating a Custom NotFound Page**: How to design a custom NotFound page that informs users of the issue.
- **Configuring Routing to Handle NotFound**: Setting up your router to direct users to the NotFound page when an invalid URL is accessed.
- **Providing Navigation Options**: Offering users options to navigate back to a valid route or the home page.

Content Example:

1. **Creating a Custom NotFound Page**:

```razor
Copy code
@page "/404"
<h3>Page Not Found</h3>
<p>Sorry, we couldn't find that page.</p>
```

1. **Configuring the Router**:

```razor
Copy code
<NotFound>
    <LayoutView Layout="@typeof(MainLayout)">
        <RedirectToPage />
    </LayoutView>
</NotFound>
```

1. **Providing Navigation Options**:

```razor
Copy code
<NavLink href="/">Go to Home</NavLink>
```

9.9 Programmatic Navigation and URL Manipulation

Programmatic navigation allows for greater control over the user experience, enabling developers to navigate based on application logic. This section explores how to implement programmatic navigation and manipulate URLs.

Subtopics to Cover:

- **Using NavigationManager for Programmatic Navigation**: How to navigate based on user actions or application state changes.
- **Manipulating Query Strings and URL Parameters**: Techniques for adding, modifying, or removing query parameters in the URL.
- **Listening to Navigation Events**: Handling navigation events for logging or state management.

Content Example:

1. Using NavigationManager:

```csharp
Copy code
@inject NavigationManager Navigation

private void NavigateToDetails(int id)
{
    Navigation.NavigateTo($"/product/{id}");
}
```

1. Manipulating Query Strings:

```csharp
Copy code
var uri = new Uri(Navigation.Uri);
var query = HttpUtility.ParseQueryString(uri.Query);
query["filter"] = "active";
Navigation.NavigateTo($"{uri.AbsolutePath}?{query}");
```

1. Listening to Navigation Events:

```csharp
Copy code
Navigation.LocationChanged += (sender, args) =>
{
    // Handle navigation event
};
```

9.10 Best Practices for Routing and Navigation in Blazor

Implementing effective routing and navigation is crucial for providing a smooth user experience. This section outlines best practices to consider when managing routing in Blazor Server applications.

Subtopics to Cover:

- **Organizing Route Structure**: Tips for structuring routes logically to enhance maintainability.
- **Consistent UI Navigation**: Ensuring navigation links are consistently styled and positioned across the application.
- **Handling Route Changes**: Implementing logic to manage state when routes change or components are updated.
- **Testing Navigation Logic**: Best practices for testing routing and navigation to ensure expected behaviors.

Content Example:

1. **Organizing Routes**:

- Use a structured approach to define routes and their hierarchy.

1. **Consistent UI**:

- Ensure that navigation components maintain a consistent design throughout the application.

1. **Testing Navigation**:

- Use unit tests to validate routing logic and user flows.

Conclusion

By the end of Chapter 9, readers will have a thorough understanding of routing and navigation in Blazor Server applications. They will learn how to implement basic and advanced routing techniques, manage navigation state, and handle not found scenarios. With this knowledge, readers will be well-equipped to create user-friendly, responsive applications that provide seamless navigation experiences.

Chapter 10: Integrating Third-Party Services and APIs in Blazor Server Applications

10.1 Introduction to Third-Party Services and APIs

Integrating third-party services and APIs into your Blazor Server applications can significantly enhance functionality and user experience. Whether you're incorporating payment processing, external data sources, or authentication providers, understanding how to work with these services is essential.

- **What Are Third-Party Services?**: These are external applications or services that provide specific functionalities or data that your application can consume. Examples include payment gateways, social media APIs, and mapping services.

- **APIs (Application Programming Interfaces)**: APIs allow different software applications to communicate with each other. They define the methods and data formats that applications can use to request and exchange information.

This chapter will guide you through the process of integrating various third-party services and APIs into your Blazor Server applications, covering both common use cases and advanced techniques.

10.2 Setting Up HttpClient for API Calls

Before integrating third-party APIs, you need to set up the HttpClient in your Blazor Server application. The HttpClient class is used for sending HTTP requests and receiving HTTP responses from a resource identified by a URI.

Subtopics to Cover:

- **Configuring HttpClient in Blazor Server**: How to register HttpClient in the dependency injection container.
- **Making HTTP Requests**: Techniques for sending GET, POST, PUT, and DELETE requests using HttpClient.
- **Handling HTTP Responses**: Managing responses, including deserializing JSON data and handling errors.

Content Example:

1. **Configuring HttpClient**: In Startup.cs, register HttpClient:

```csharp
Copy code
public void ConfigureServices(IServiceCollection services)
{
    services.AddHttpClient(); // Registering HttpClient
}
```

1. **Making GET Requests**:

```csharp
Copy code
@inject HttpClient Http
```

```
private async Task<List<YourDataType>> GetData()
{
    var response = await
    Http.GetAsync("https://api.example.com/data");
    response.EnsureSuccessStatusCode();
    return await
    response.Content.ReadFromJsonAsync<List<YourDataType>>();
}
```

1. **Handling Errors**:

```csharp
Copy code
try
{
    var data = await GetData();
}
catch (HttpRequestException ex)
{
    // Handle error
}
```

10.3 Integrating RESTful APIs

RESTful APIs are among the most common types of APIs you'll encounter. This section discusses how to integrate and consume RESTful APIs in Blazor Server applications.

Subtopics to Cover:

- **Understanding REST Principles**: Overview of REST principles and how they apply to API design.
- **Consuming RESTful APIs**: Best practices for consuming REST APIs, including authentication and authorization.
- **Working with JSON Data**: Techniques for serializing and deserializing JSON data.

Content Example:

1. Consuming a RESTful API:

```csharp
Copy code
private async Task<List<Product>> GetProductsAsync()
{
    var response = await
    Http.GetAsync("https://api.example.com/products");
    response.EnsureSuccessStatusCode();
    return await response.Content.
ReadFromJsonAsync<List<Product>>();
}
```

1. Handling Authentication:

- If the API requires authentication, you can include the token in the headers:

```csharp
Copy code
Http.DefaultRequestHeaders.Authorization = new
AuthenticationHeaderValue("Bearer", "your_token_here");
```

1. Serializing JSON Data:

```csharp
Copy code
var jsonString = JsonSerializer.Serialize(product);
```

10.4 Integrating Payment Gateways

Payment gateways allow you to process online transactions securely. This section will cover the integration of a popular payment gateway API into a Blazor Server application.

Subtopics to Cover:

- **Choosing a Payment Gateway**: Overview of popular payment gateways (e.g., Stripe, PayPal).
- **Creating a Payment Component**: Building a component that handles payment processing.
- **Handling Webhooks for Payment Notifications**: Setting up webhooks to receive notifications about payment events.

Content Example:

1. **Integrating Stripe**:

- Install Stripe NuGet packages:

```bash
Copy code
Install-Package Stripe.net
```

1. **Creating a Payment Form**:

```razor
Copy code
<EditForm Model="@paymentInfo"
OnValidSubmit="ProcessPayment">
    <InputText @bind-Value="
```

```
paymentInfo.CardNumber" placeholder="Card Number" />
    <InputText @bind-Value="paymentInfo.ExpiryDate"
    placeholder="MM/YY" />
    <InputText @bind-Value="paymentInfo.Cvc" placeholder="CVC" />
    <button type="submit">Pay</button>
</EditForm>

@code {
    private PaymentInfo paymentInfo = new PaymentInfo();

    private async Task ProcessPayment()
    {
        // Call Stripe API to process payment
    }
}
```

1. **Handling Webhooks**:

- Set up an endpoint to receive Stripe webhook events and handle them appropriately.

10.5 Using Social Media APIs

Integrating social media APIs allows users to interact with platforms like Facebook, Twitter, and Instagram directly from your application. This section will guide you through the process of using a social media API.

Subtopics to Cover:

- **Authentication with Social Media APIs**: How to authenticate users via OAuth with social media platforms.
- **Posting and Retrieving Content**: Techniques for posting updates and retrieving user content.
- **Handling Rate Limiting**: Strategies for managing API rate limits and avoiding throttling.

Content Example:

1. **Authenticating with Facebook**:

- Use Facebook's SDK or OAuth flow to obtain an access token.

1. **Posting Content**:

```csharp
Copy code
private async Task PostToFacebook(string message)
{
    var response = await Http.PostAsJsonAsync("https://graph.
facebook.com/me/feed", new { message = message });
    response.EnsureSuccessStatusCode();
}
```

1. **Handling Rate Limits**:

- Monitor API responses for rate limit headers and implement backoff strategies.

10.6 Integrating Mapping Services

Mapping services such as Google Maps or Mapbox provide geolocation functionalities and mapping capabilities. This section discusses how to integrate mapping services into Blazor Server applications.

Subtopics to Cover:

- **Choosing a Mapping Service**: Overview of popular mapping services and their features.
- **Displaying Maps in Blazor**: How to render maps within a Blazor component.
- **Handling Map Events**: Techniques for responding to user interactions with the map.

Content Example:

1. **Integrating Google Maps:**

- Add the Google Maps API script to your _Host.cshtml:

```html
html
Copy code
<script async defer src="https:
//maps.googleapis.com/maps/api/
js?key=YOUR_API_
KEY&callback=initMap"></script>
```

1. **Displaying a Map:**

```razor
razor
Copy code
<div id="map" style="height: 400px; width: 100%;"></div>

@code {
    private void InitMap()
    {
        // Initialize the map
    }
}
```

1. **Handling Map Events:**

```javascript
javascript
Copy code
```

```
function initMap() {
    var map = new google.maps.Map(
document.getElementById('map'),
{ zoom: 8, center: { lat: -34.397, lng: 150.644 } });
    map.addListener('click', function (event) {
        // Handle click event
    });
}
```

10.7 Integrating Email Services

Email services like SendGrid or SMTP can be integrated into your Blazor Server applications for sending notifications, confirmations, and newsletters. This section explains how to set up and use an email service.

Subtopics to Cover:

- **Choosing an Email Service Provider**: Overview of popular email services and their features.
- **Configuring Email Settings**: How to set up SMTP settings or API keys.
- **Sending Emails from Blazor**: Implementing functionality to send emails based on user actions or events.

Content Example:

1. **Integrating SendGrid**:

- Install the SendGrid NuGet package:

```bash
Copy code
Install-Package SendGrid
```

1. **Configuring Email Settings**:

```csharp
Copy code
public class EmailService
{
    private readonly SendGridClient _client;

    public EmailService(string apiKey)
    {
        _client = new SendGridClient(apiKey);
    }

    public async Task SendEmailAsync
(string toEmail, string subject, string message)
    {
        var from = new EmailAddress
("noreply@example.com", "Example App");
        var to = new EmailAddress(toEmail);
        var msg = MailHelper.
CreateSingleEmail(from, to, subject, message, message);
        await _client.SendEmailAsync(msg);
    }
}
```

Chapter 11: Building and Consuming APIs in Blazor Server Applications

11.1 Introduction to APIs

APIs (Application Programming Interfaces) are essential for enabling communication between different software applications. They allow developers to build applications that can interact with external services or expose their functionality to other applications. In a Blazor Server application, building and consuming APIs is crucial for creating rich, interactive applications that can leverage data from various sources.

- **What is an API?**: An API defines a set of rules and protocols for building software applications. It allows different systems to communicate and share data.
- **Types of APIs**: This section will briefly touch on different types of APIs, including REST, SOAP, and GraphQL, with a focus on RESTful APIs, which are commonly used in web applications.

This chapter will guide you through the process of building APIs within your Blazor Server application and consuming external APIs to integrate various functionalities.

11.2 Setting Up ASP.NET Core Web API

To build APIs in a Blazor Server application, you will typically set up

ASP.NET Core Web API services. This section discusses how to configure your project to create a Web API.

Subtopics to Cover:

- **Creating an API Controller**: How to create an API controller in your Blazor Server project.
- **Defining API Endpoints**: Setting up routes for your API endpoints using attributes.
- **Configuring Services in Startup**: Registering services and middleware required for API functionality in your Startup.cs.

Content Example:

1. **Creating an API Controller**:

```csharp
Copy code
using Microsoft.AspNetCore.Mvc;

[Route("api/[controller]")]
[ApiController]
public class ProductsController : ControllerBase
{
    private readonly IProductService _productService;

    public ProductsController(IProductService productService)
    {
        _productService = productService;
    }

    // GET: api/products
    [HttpGet]
    public async Task<ActionResult<IEnumerable<Product>>>
    GetProducts()
    {
```

```
        return await _productService.GetProductsAsync();
    }
}
```

1. **Defining API Endpoints**:

```csharp
csharp
Copy code
[HttpGet("{id:int}")]
public async Task<ActionResult<Product>> GetProduct(int id)
{
    var product = await _productService.GetProductByIdAsync(id);
    if (product == null)
    {
        return NotFound();
    }
    return product;
}
```

1. **Configuring Services in Startup**:

```csharp
csharp
Copy code
public void ConfigureServices(IServiceCollection services)
{
    services.AddControllers();
    services.AddScoped<IProductService, ProductService>();
}
```

11.3 Creating CRUD Operations for Your API

In this section, you will implement CRUD (Create, Read, Update, Delete) operations for your API. This is essential for managing resources in your application.

Subtopics to Cover:

- **Creating New Resources**: How to implement the POST method to create new records.
- **Reading Resources**: Using GET requests to retrieve data.
- **Updating Resources**: Implementing PUT or PATCH methods to update existing records.
- **Deleting Resources**: How to implement the DELETE method to remove records.

Content Example:

1. **Creating New Resources**:

```csharp
Copy code
[HttpPost]
public async Task<ActionResult<Product>> CreateProduct(Product
product)
{
    await _productService.CreateProductAsync(product);
    return CreatedAtAction(nameof(GetProduct), new { id =
    product.Id }, product);
}
```

1. **Updating Resources**:

```csharp
Copy code
[HttpPut("{id:int}")]
public async Task<IActionResult> UpdateProduct(int id, Product
```

```csharp
product)
{
    if (id != product.Id)
    {
        return BadRequest();
    }
    await _productService.UpdateProductAsync(product);
    return NoContent();
}
```

1. Deleting Resources:

```
csharp
Copy code
[HttpDelete("{id:int}")]
public async Task<IActionResult> DeleteProduct(int id)
{
    await _productService.DeleteProductAsync(id);
    return NoContent();
}
```

11.4 Testing Your API with Postman

After building your API, it is essential to test its endpoints to ensure they function correctly. Postman is a powerful tool for testing APIs.

Subtopics to Cover:

- **Setting Up Postman**: How to install and configure Postman for API testing.
- **Creating Requests**: How to create GET, POST, PUT, and DELETE requests in Postman.
- **Viewing Responses**: Understanding how to analyze responses and troubleshoot issues.

Content Example:

1. **Setting Up Postman**:

- Download and install Postman from the official website.

1. **Creating a GET Request**:

- Enter the URL https://localhost:5001/api/products and click Send to retrieve the list of products.

1. **Viewing Responses**:

- Analyze the response body and status code to verify that the API is functioning correctly.

11.5 Consuming External APIs in Blazor Server

In addition to building your APIs, you may need to consume external APIs to leverage third-party services. This section discusses how to make HTTP requests to external APIs and handle the responses.

Subtopics to Cover:

- **Making HTTP Requests**: How to send GET, POST, and other requests to external APIs using HttpClient.
- **Handling API Responses**: Techniques for parsing and handling JSON responses from APIs.
- **Error Handling and Retries**: Strategies for managing errors when consuming external APIs.

Content Example:

1. **Making a GET Request to an External API**:

```csharp
Copy code
private async Task<List<ExternalDataType>> GetExternalDataAsync()
{
    var response = await
    Http.GetAsync("https://api.example.com/data");
    response.EnsureSuccessStatusCode();
    return await
    response.Content.ReadFromJsonAsync<List<ExternalDataType>>();
}
```

1. Handling API Responses:

```csharp
Copy code
var data = await GetExternalDataAsync();
foreach (var item in data)
{
    // Process each item
}
```

1. Error Handling:

```csharp
Copy code
try
{
    var data = await GetExternalDataAsync();
}
catch (HttpRequestException ex)
```

```
{
    // Log and handle the error
}
```

11.6 Authentication and Authorization with APIs

When working with external APIs, authentication and authorization are often required to secure access. This section covers how to implement authentication for both your APIs and external APIs.

Subtopics to Cover:

- **Using JWT for Authentication**: How to implement JSON Web Tokens for securing API access.
- **Integrating OAuth for External APIs**: How to authenticate with external APIs using OAuth 2.0.
- **Protecting Your APIs**: Implementing authorization policies to secure your own APIs.

Content Example:

1. **Using JWT for Authentication**:

```csharp
Copy code
public string GenerateJwtToken(User user)
{
    // Generate JWT token logic
}
```

1. **Integrating OAuth**:

- Redirect users to the OAuth provider's login page and obtain an access token.

1. **Protecting Your APIs**:

```csharp
Copy code
[Authorize]
[HttpGet("secure-data")]
public IActionResult GetSecureData()
{
    // Return secure data
}
```

11.7 Error Handling and Logging in APIs

Effective error handling and logging are essential for maintaining API reliability and aiding in troubleshooting. This section discusses strategies for managing errors in your APIs and logging activities for diagnostics.

Subtopics to Cover:

- **Global Error Handling**: Implementing middleware for global error handling in your API.
- **Returning Meaningful Error Responses**: How to structure error responses to provide clear information to the client.
- **Implementing Logging**: Using logging frameworks to record API activities and errors.

Content Example:

1. **Global Error Handling**:

```csharp
Copy code
public void Configure(IApplicationBuilder app)
{
    app.UseMiddleware<ErrorHandlingMiddleware>();
```

```
}

public class ErrorHandlingMiddleware
{
    public async Task Invoke(HttpContext context)
    {
        try
        {
            await _next(context);
        }
        catch (Exception ex)
        {
            await HandleExceptionAsync(context, ex);
        }
    }
}
```

1. **Returning Meaningful Error Responses**:

```csharp
csharp
Copy code
private Task HandleExceptionAsync(HttpContext context, Exception
ex)
{
    context.Response.ContentType = "application/json";
    context.Response.StatusCode =
    (int)HttpStatusCode.InternalServerError;
    return context.Response.WriteAsync(new
    {
        StatusCode = context.Response.StatusCode,
        Message = ex.Message
    }.ToString());
}
```

1. **Implementing Logging**:

```
csharp
Copy code
public void ConfigureServices(IServiceCollection services)
{
    services.AddLogging();
}
```

11.8 Versioning Your APIs

API versioning is important to manage changes and updates without disrupting existing clients. This section covers strategies for implementing API versioning in your Blazor Server application.

Subtopics to Cover:

- **Why Versioning is Important**: Understanding the necessity of versioning for API stability.
- **Implementing Versioning Strategies**: Common approaches to API versioning, such as URL path versioning, query string versioning, and header versioning.
- **Handling Versioned API Requests**: How to manage requests for different API versions.

Content Example:

1. **Implementing URL Path Versioning**:

```
csharp
Copy code
[Route("api/v1/products")]
public class ProductsV1Controller : ControllerBase
{
    // API V1 methods
}
```

1. **Handling Versioned Requests**:

```csharp
Copy code
[HttpGet]
public ActionResult<IEnumerable<Product>> GetProducts(string
version)
{
    if (version == "v1")
    {
        // Handle V1 logic
    }
    else
    {
        // Handle latest logic
    }
}
```

11.9 Testing Your APIs

Testing is crucial for ensuring that your APIs function correctly and meet user expectations. This section discusses various approaches to testing your APIs, including unit tests, integration tests, and automated testing tools.

Subtopics to Cover:

- **Writing Unit Tests for API Endpoints**: How to write unit tests to validate the behavior of your API endpoints.
- **Integration Testing**: Techniques for testing your API in conjunction with other parts of your application.
- **Using Automated Testing Tools**: Overview of tools like Postman and Swagger for testing your APIs.

Content Example:

1. **Writing Unit Tests**:

```csharp
csharp
Copy code
[Fact]
public async Task GetProducts_ReturnsOkResult()
{
    // Arrange
    var controller = new ProductsController(mockService.Object);

    // Act
    var result = await controller.GetProducts();

    // Assert
    var okResult = Assert.IsType<OkObjectResult>(result);
    var products = Assert.IsType<List<Product>>(okResult.Value);
}
```

1. **Integration Testing**:

- Set up an in-memory database to test the API's interactions with the data layer.

1. **Using Postman for Testing**:

- Create collections in Postman to automate and document your API tests.

11.10 Best Practices for Building and Consuming APIs

To ensure the reliability, maintainability, and usability of your APIs, it is essential to follow best practices. This section outlines key recommendations for building and consuming APIs effectively.

Subtopics to Cover:

- **Designing RESTful APIs**: Best practices for designing clean and effective RESTful APIs.

- **Implementing Security Best Practices**: Ensuring your APIs are secure against common vulnerabilities.
- **Versioning and Documentation**: Strategies for documenting your APIs and managing versions.
- **Monitoring and Performance Optimization**: Techniques for monitoring API performance and optimizing response times.

Content Example:

1. **Designing RESTful APIs**:

- Use clear and consistent naming conventions for endpoints.
- Follow HTTP methods (GET, POST, PUT, DELETE) correctly based on the action performed.

1. **Implementing Security**:

- Use HTTPS for secure communication.
- Implement authentication and authorization properly.

1. **Versioning and Documentation**:

- Utilize tools like Swagger/OpenAPI for documenting your API endpoints.
- Clearly communicate breaking changes in version updates.

Conclusion

By the end of Chapter 11, readers will have a comprehensive understanding of how to build and consume APIs in Blazor Server applications. They will learn how to set up ASP.NET Core Web API, implement CRUD operations, consume external APIs, and manage authentication and error handling. With this knowledge, readers will be well-equipped to enhance their Blazor applications with robust API integrations, enabling richer functionalities and seamless user experiences.

Chapter 12: Deploying Blazor Server Applications

12.1 Introduction to Deployment

Deployment is the process of making your Blazor Server application available to users on the internet. It involves transferring your application code to a web server, configuring the server environment, and ensuring that everything runs smoothly. Understanding deployment is crucial for getting your application into the hands of users and maintaining its performance and security.

- **Why Deployment Matters**: Successful deployment ensures that your application is accessible, secure, and performs well. It is also essential for integrating updates and managing user data.
- **Overview of Deployment Options**: This chapter will discuss various deployment options available for Blazor Server applications, including cloud hosting, on-premises hosting, and containers.

12.2 Preparing Your Blazor Server Application for Deployment

Before deploying your application, you need to ensure that it is properly configured for production. This section covers key preparations for deployment.

Subtopics to Cover:

- **Configuration Settings**: How to adjust configuration settings for production, including connection strings and API keys.
- **Logging and Error Handling**: Setting up logging and error handling for production to monitor application health.
- **Performance Optimization**: Techniques for optimizing performance, such as enabling response compression and configuring caching.

Content Example:

1. **Configuration Settings**: In appsettings.Production.json, specify production settings:

```json
Copy code
{
    "ConnectionStrings": {
        "DefaultConnection":
        "Server=productionserver;Database=MyDb;User
        Id=myuser;Password=mypassword;"
    }
}
```

1. **Logging and Error Handling**: Configure logging in Startup.cs:

```csharp
Copy code
public void Configure(IApplicationBuilder app,
 IWebHostEnvironment env)
{
    if (env.IsDevelopment())
    {
        app.UseDeveloperExceptionPage();
    }
```

```
else
{
    app.UseExceptionHandler("/Error");
    app.UseHsts();
}

app.UseHttpsRedirection();
app.UseStaticFiles();
app.UseRouting();
app.UseAuthorization();
}
```

1. **Performance Optimization**: Enable response compression:

```csharp
Copy code
services.AddResponseCompression(options =>
{
    options.EnableForHttps = true;
});
```

12.3 Hosting Options for Blazor Server Applications

Choosing the right hosting environment is crucial for your application's performance and scalability. This section discusses various hosting options for Blazor Server applications.

Subtopics to Cover:

- **Cloud Hosting Providers**: Overview of popular cloud hosting providers like Azure, AWS, and Google Cloud.
- **On-Premises Hosting**: Considerations for hosting on local servers, including IIS and Docker.
- **Containerization with Docker**: How to containerize your Blazor Server application using Docker for easier deployment and management.

Content Example:

1. **Cloud Hosting with Azure**:

- Create an Azure App Service and configure it to host your Blazor Server application.

1. **On-Premises Hosting with IIS**:

- Set up IIS to host your application, including configuring application pools and sites.

1. **Dockerizing Your Application**: Create a Dockerfile:

```dockerfile
Copy code
FROM mcr.microsoft.com/dotnet/aspnet:6.0 AS base
WORKDIR /app
EXPOSE 80

FROM mcr.microsoft.com/dotnet/sdk:6.0 AS build
WORKDIR /src
COPY ["MyBlazorApp/MyBlazorApp.csproj", "MyBlazorApp/"]
RUN dotnet restore "MyBlazorApp/MyBlazorApp.csproj"
COPY . .
WORKDIR "/src/MyBlazorApp"
RUN dotnet build "MyBlazorApp.csproj"
 -c Release -o /app/build

FROM build AS publish
RUN dotnet publish "MyBlazorApp.csproj"
 -c Release -o /app/publish

FROM base AS final
WORKDIR /app
```

```
COPY --from=publish /app/publish .
ENTRYPOINT ["dotnet", "MyBlazorApp.dll"]
```

12.4 Deploying to Azure App Service

Azure App Service provides a powerful platform for hosting web applications. This section covers the step-by-step process of deploying a Blazor Server application to Azure.

Subtopics to Cover:

- **Creating an Azure App Service**: How to create and configure an App Service in the Azure portal.
- **Publishing from Visual Studio**: Using Visual Studio's built-in publishing tools to deploy your application to Azure.
- **Managing Application Settings**: Configuring application settings and connection strings in the Azure portal.

Content Example:

1. **Creating an Azure App Service**:

- Navigate to the Azure portal, select "Create a resource", then "Web App".
- Fill in the required fields, such as resource group, app name, and runtime stack.

1. **Publishing from Visual Studio**:

- Right-click your project in Visual Studio and select "Publish".
- Choose "Azure" as the target and follow the prompts to complete the deployment.

1. **Managing Application Settings**: In the Azure portal, navigate to your App Service and select "Configuration" to add or modify application settings.

12.5 Deploying to AWS Elastic Beanstalk

AWS Elastic Beanstalk is another popular cloud hosting option. This section discusses how to deploy your Blazor Server application to AWS.

Subtopics to Cover:

- **Setting Up AWS Elastic Beanstalk**: How to create an Elastic Beanstalk environment for your application.
- **Packaging Your Application**: Preparing your Blazor Server application for deployment to Elastic Beanstalk.
- **Monitoring and Managing Your Application**: Using the AWS management console to monitor application performance and manage resources.

Content Example:

1. **Setting Up Elastic Beanstalk**:

- Go to the AWS Management Console, select Elastic Beanstalk, and create a new application.
- Configure the environment settings, including platform and instance type.

1. **Packaging Your Application**:

- Use the AWS Toolkit for Visual Studio to publish directly to Elastic Beanstalk or package your application as a ZIP file for upload.

1. **Monitoring Your Application**:

- Use the Elastic Beanstalk console to monitor application health and logs.

12.6 Deploying to a Local IIS Server

For applications that need to be hosted on-premises, IIS (Internet Information Services) provides a robust solution. This section covers how to deploy your Blazor Server application to an IIS server.

Subtopics to Cover:

- **Setting Up IIS for Hosting**: Configuring IIS to host ASP.NET Core applications.
- **Publishing from Visual Studio**: How to publish your Blazor application directly to the IIS server.
- **Configuring Application Pools and Settings**: Setting up application pools and configuring settings for your application.

Content Example:

1. **Setting Up IIS**:

- Ensure that IIS is installed on your server and that ASP.NET Core Hosting Bundle is configured.
- Open IIS Manager and create a new site pointing to your Blazor application's publish folder.

1. **Publishing to IIS**:

- In Visual Studio, right-click your project, select "Publish", and choose the folder option to publish to your IIS directory.

1. **Configuring Application Pools**:

- Set the application pool to use the .NET CLR version "No Managed Code" since Blazor Server runs on .NET Core.

12.7 Continuous Deployment with CI/CD Pipelines

Implementing Continuous Integration and Continuous Deployment (CI/CD) allows for automated testing and deployment of your Blazor Server applications. This section discusses setting up CI/CD pipelines using popular services.

Subtopics to Cover:

- **Using GitHub Actions for CI/CD**: How to set up GitHub Actions to automate the build and deployment process.
- **Implementing Azure DevOps Pipelines**: Configuring Azure DevOps pipelines for CI/CD.
- **Best Practices for CI/CD**: Key considerations and practices for maintaining effective CI/CD workflows.

Content Example:

1. **Using GitHub Actions**: Create a .github/workflows/deploy.yml file:

```yaml
yaml
Copy code
name: Deploy Blazor Server

on:
  push:
    branches:
      - main

jobs:
  build-and-deploy:
    runs-on: ubuntu-latest
    steps:
      - name: Checkout code
        uses: actions/checkout@v2

      - name: Setup .NET
        uses: actions/setup-dotnet@v1
        with:
          dotnet-version: '6.0.x'
```

```
      - name: Restore dependencies
        run: dotnet restore

      - name: Build
        run: dotnet build --configuration Release

      - name: Publish
        run: dotnet publish
--configuration Release --output ./publish

      - name: Deploy to Azure Web App
        uses: azure/webapps-deploy@v2
        with:
          app-name: 'YourAppName'
          publish-profile: ${{
secrets.AZURE_WEBAPP_PUBLISH_PROFILE }}

          package: './publish'
```

1. **Implementing Azure DevOps Pipelines**:

- Set up a new pipeline in Azure DevOps and link it to your repository.
- Define build and release pipelines using the visual editor or YAML files.

1. **Best Practices for CI/CD**:

- Ensure all tests pass before deploying to production.
- Use separate environments for development, testing, and production.

12.8 Securing Your Deployed Application

Security is a critical aspect of deploying applications. This section covers best practices for securing your Blazor Server application in production.

Subtopics to Cover:

- **Using HTTPS**: How to enforce HTTPS to secure data in transit.
- **Implementing Authentication and Authorization**: Ensuring proper authentication and authorization mechanisms are in place.
- **Configuring Firewalls and Access Controls**: Best practices for setting up firewalls and controlling access to your application.

Content Example:

1. **Enforcing HTTPS**: In Startup.cs, add:

```csharp
Copy code
app.UseHttpsRedirection();
```

1. **Implementing Authentication**: Ensure that your APIs require authentication and use secure tokens.
2. **Configuring Firewalls**:

- Set up network security groups and firewalls to limit access to your application.

12.9 Monitoring and Maintaining Your Application

After deployment, monitoring and maintenance are crucial to ensure the application runs smoothly. This section discusses tools and techniques for monitoring your Blazor Server application.

Subtopics to Cover:

- **Using Application Insights**: Integrating Application Insights for monitoring performance and errors.
- **Setting Up Logging**: Configuring logging to capture application events and errors.

- **Regular Updates and Maintenance**: Best practices for maintaining your application and applying updates.

Content Example:

1. **Using Application Insights**: Install the Application Insights SDK:

```bash
Copy code
Install-Package Microsoft.ApplicationInsights.AspNetCore
```

1. Configure Application Insights in Startup.cs:

```csharp
Copy code
services.AddApplicationInsightsTelemetry(
Configuration[
"ApplicationInsights:InstrumentationKey"]);
```

1. **Setting Up Logging**: Use built-in logging to capture important events:

```csharp
Copy code
public void Configure(IApplicationBuilder
app, IWebHostEnvironment env, ILogger<Startup> logger)
{
    app.Use(async (context, next) =>
    {
        logger.LogInformation("Handling request: " +
        context.Request.Path);
```

```
        await next.Invoke();
        logger.LogInformation
("Finished handling request.");
    });
}
```

1. **Regular Updates**:

- Schedule regular reviews of dependencies and application code to apply updates.

12.10 Best Practices for Deploying Blazor Server Applications

To ensure successful deployment and maintain a healthy application, following best practices is essential. This section outlines key recommendations for deploying Blazor Server applications.

Subtopics to Cover:

- **Consistent Build and Release Processes**: Use CI/CD pipelines for consistent builds and releases.
- **Environment-Specific Configurations**: Maintain different configurations for development, staging, and production environments.
- **Testing Before Deployment**: Ensure thorough testing of your application in a staging environment before deploying to production.
- **Documentation**: Maintain clear documentation for your deployment process and configurations.

Content Example:

1. **Consistent Processes**:

- Define standard operating procedures for builds and releases.

1. **Environment Configurations**: Use environment variables to manage settings specific to each environment.
2. **Testing and Documentation**: Document your deployment steps and update them regularly as processes change.

Conclusion

By the end of Chapter 12, readers will have a comprehensive understanding of how to deploy Blazor Server applications effectively. They will learn about various deployment options, preparing applications for production, securing deployed applications, and monitoring their performance. With this knowledge, readers will be equipped to take their Blazor applications from development to production, ensuring a smooth transition and ongoing reliability.

Chapter 13: Building Responsive User Interfaces with CSS and Blazor Server

13.1 Introduction to Responsive Design

Responsive design is an essential aspect of modern web development, ensuring that applications function and look great across a variety of devices and screen sizes. In Blazor Server, incorporating responsive design principles enhances user experience and accessibility.

- **What is Responsive Design?**: Responsive design is an approach that allows web applications to adapt their layout and appearance based on the screen size and resolution of the device being used.
- **Importance of Responsive Design**: With the growing use of mobile devices, ensuring that applications are user-friendly on all platforms is crucial for engagement and retention.

This chapter will guide you through the process of building responsive user interfaces in Blazor Server applications, leveraging CSS for styling and layout adjustments.

13.2 Setting Up Your Blazor Server Project

Before diving into responsive design, you need to set up your Blazor Server project with the necessary files and configurations. This section covers the initial setup.

Subtopics to Cover:

- **Creating a New Blazor Server Project**: How to create a new Blazor Server project in Visual Studio.
- **Adding CSS Frameworks**: Introduction to popular CSS frameworks like Bootstrap, Tailwind CSS, and Bulma, and how to integrate them into your project.
- **Organizing Your Stylesheets**: Best practices for structuring your CSS files and managing styles.

Content Example:

1. **Creating a New Blazor Server Project**:

- Open Visual Studio and select "Create a new project".
- Choose "Blazor App" and select "Blazor Server App".

1. **Adding Bootstrap**:

- Include Bootstrap via CDN in the _Host.cshtml file:

```html
Copy code
<link rel="stylesheet" href="https://maxcdn.bootstrapcdn
.com/bootstrap/5.1.3/css/bootstrap.min.css">
```

1. **Organizing Your Stylesheets**:

- Create a css folder in your project and include custom stylesheets for better organization.

13.3 Understanding CSS Basics

To effectively build responsive user interfaces, a solid understanding of CSS is necessary. This section covers the foundational concepts of CSS.

Subtopics to Cover:

- **CSS Selectors and Properties**: Overview of various selectors and properties that you can use to style your components.
- **Box Model and Layout**: Understanding the CSS box model and how it affects layout design.
- **Flexbox and Grid Layouts**: Introduction to Flexbox and CSS Grid, powerful layout models for creating responsive designs.

Content Example:

1. **CSS Selectors**:

```css
Copy code
/* Class selector */
.my-class {
    color: blue;
}

/* ID selector */
#my-id {
    font-size: 20px;
}
```

1. **Box Model**:

- Understanding margin, border, padding, and content dimensions.

1. **Flexbox Example**:

```css
css
Copy code
.flex-container {
    display: flex;
    justify-content: space-around;
}
```

13.4 Building a Responsive Navigation Menu

A responsive navigation menu is critical for any web application. This section covers how to create a navigation menu that adapts to different screen sizes.

Subtopics to Cover:

- **Creating a Basic Navigation Menu**: How to build a simple navigation menu using Bootstrap classes.
- **Making the Menu Responsive**: Implementing responsive features such as collapsing the menu on smaller screens.
- **Styling the Navigation Menu**: Customizing the appearance of the navigation menu with CSS.

Content Example:

1. **Basic Navigation Menu**:

```razor
razor
Copy code
<nav class="navbar navbar-expand-lg navbar-light bg-light">
    <a class="navbar-brand" href="#">My App</a>
    <button class="navbar-toggler" type="button"
    data-bs-toggle="collapse" data-bs-target="#navbarNav"
    aria-controls="navbarNav" aria-expanded="false"
    aria-label="Toggle navigation">
        <span class="navbar-toggler-icon"></span>
```

```
    </button>
    <div class="collapse navbar-collapse" id="navbarNav">
        <ul class="navbar-nav">
            <li class="nav-item">
                <NavLink class="nav-link" href="/">Home</NavLink>
            </li>
            <li class="nav-item">
                <NavLink class="nav-link"
                href="/about">About</NavLink>
            </li>
        </ul>
    </div>
</nav>
```

1. **Responsive Features**:

• Use Bootstrap's responsive classes to manage visibility and layout.

1. **Custom Styling**:

```css
Copy code
.navbar {
    background-color: #f8f9fa;
}
```

13.5 Creating Responsive Forms

Forms are essential for user interaction, and creating responsive forms ensures that they are usable on all devices. This section covers best practices for building responsive forms in Blazor.

Subtopics to Cover:

• **Building Basic Forms**: How to create a basic form using Blazor components and Bootstrap.

- **Responsive Input Fields**: Techniques for styling input fields to be responsive.
- **Validation and Feedback**: Implementing validation and providing user feedback in a responsive manner.

Content Example:

1. Building Basic Forms:

```razor
Copy code
<EditForm Model="@user" OnValidSubmit="HandleValidSubmit">
    <DataAnnotationsValidator />
    <ValidationSummary />
    <div class="mb-3">
        <label for="name" class="form-label">Name</label>
        <InputText id="name" class="form-control"
        @bind-Value="user.Name" />
    </div>
    <button type="submit" class="btn
 btn-primary">Submit</button>
</EditForm>
```

1. Responsive Input Fields:

- Utilize Bootstrap's grid system to ensure that input fields resize appropriately.

1. Validation Feedback:

```razor
Copy code
```

```
<ValidationMessage For="@(() => user.Name)"
 class="text-danger" />
```

13.6 Implementing Responsive Grids and Layouts

Using CSS Grid and Flexbox, you can create complex and responsive layouts. This section explores how to implement grid-based layouts in your Blazor applications.

Subtopics to Cover:

- **Creating a CSS Grid Layout**: How to use CSS Grid to structure your application's layout.
- **Flexbox for Responsive Design**: Leveraging Flexbox for more dynamic and flexible layouts.
- **Combining Grid and Flexbox**: Techniques for combining both models for advanced layouts.

Content Example:

1. **Creating a CSS Grid Layout**:

```css
css
Copy code
.grid-container {
    display: grid;
    grid-template-columns: repeat(auto-fill, minmax(200px, 1fr));
    gap: 10px;
}
```

1. **Flexbox Layout Example**:

```css
css
Copy code
.flex-container {
    display: flex;
    flex-wrap: wrap;
    justify-content: space-between;
}
```

1. **Combining Grid and Flexbox**:

```html
html
Copy code
<div class="grid-container">
    <div class="flex-container">
        <!-- Flex items -->
    </div>
</div>
```

13.7 Media Queries for Responsive Design

Media queries allow you to apply different styles based on the viewport size. This section discusses how to implement media queries in your Blazor applications.

Subtopics to Cover:

- **Understanding Media Queries**: How media queries work and their syntax.
- **Creating Breakpoints**: Defining breakpoints for responsive design.
- **Applying Styles with Media Queries**: Techniques for using media queries to adjust styles for different devices.

Content Example:

1. **Basic Media Query Syntax**:

```css
css
Copy code
@media (max-width: 600px) {
    .responsive-class {
        font-size: 14px;
    }
}
```

1. **Creating Breakpoints**:

- Define breakpoints for different screen sizes, such as mobile, tablet, and desktop.

1. **Applying Styles**:

```css
css
Copy code
@media (max-width: 768px) {
    .navbar {
        flex-direction: column;
    }
}
```

13.8 Using CSS Frameworks for Faster Development

CSS frameworks like Bootstrap, Tailwind CSS, and Foundation can accelerate development and help you maintain consistent styles. This section discusses how to leverage CSS frameworks effectively.

Subtopics to Cover:

- **Choosing a CSS Framework**: Overview of popular CSS frameworks and their advantages.
- **Integrating a CSS Framework**: How to add a CSS framework to your

Blazor project.

- **Utilizing Framework Features**: Techniques for using built-in features and components of the framework.

Content Example:

1. **Choosing a CSS Framework**:

- Compare the features of Bootstrap and Tailwind CSS, and decide which suits your needs.

1. **Integrating Bootstrap**:

- Add the Bootstrap CDN in your _Host.cshtml.

1. **Utilizing Framework Features**:

- Use Bootstrap classes for buttons, forms, and grids:

```html
Copy code
<button class="btn btn-primary">Click Me</button>
```

13.9 Custom Styling for Unique Branding

While CSS frameworks provide a foundation, customizing styles is essential for branding. This section covers how to apply custom styles to create a unique look for your Blazor application.

Subtopics to Cover:

- **Creating a Custom Stylesheet**: Best practices for writing custom CSS.
- **Overriding Framework Styles**: Techniques for overriding default styles from frameworks.

- **Using Variables and Mixins**: Leveraging CSS variables and preprocessors like SASS or LESS for better style management.

Content Example:

1. **Creating a Custom Stylesheet**:

- Create a file called custom.css and link it in _Host.cshtml.

1. **Overriding Styles**:

```css
Copy code
.btn-primary {
    background-color: #007bff; /* Custom blue */
    border-color: #007bff;
}
```

1. **Using CSS Variables**:

```css
Copy code
:root {
    --main-color: #007bff;
}

.btn-primary {
    background-color: var(--main-color);
}
```

13.10 Accessibility in Responsive Design

Ensuring your application is accessible is crucial for inclusivity. This section discusses how to implement accessibility features in your responsive

152

design.

Subtopics to Cover:

- **Understanding Accessibility Standards**: Overview of WCAG (Web Content Accessibility Guidelines).
- **Implementing ARIA Roles and Attributes**: How to use ARIA to enhance accessibility.
- **Testing for Accessibility**: Techniques for testing and validating your application's accessibility.

Content Example:

1. **Understanding Accessibility Standards**:

- Familiarize yourself with WCAG principles such as perceivable, operable, understandable, and robust.

1. **Implementing ARIA**:

```html
Copy code
<button aria-label="Close" class="btn-close">X</button>
```

1. **Testing for Accessibility**:

- Use tools like Axe or Lighthouse to audit your application for accessibility compliance.

13.11 Finalizing and Testing Your User Interface

After implementing responsive design and accessibility features, it's essential to test your user interface thoroughly. This section discusses best practices for finalizing and testing your UI.

Subtopics to Cover:

- **Cross-Browser Testing**: Techniques for ensuring compatibility across different browsers.
- **Mobile Device Testing**: Tools and methods for testing your application on various mobile devices.
- **User Testing and Feedback**: Gathering user feedback to improve the UI based on real-world usage.

Content Example:

1. **Cross-Browser Testing**:

- Use tools like BrowserStack to test your application across different browsers.

1. **Mobile Device Testing**:

- Test on physical devices and use responsive design mode in browser dev tools.

1. **User Testing**:

- Conduct user testing sessions to gather feedback on usability and aesthetics.

Conclusion

By the end of Chapter 13, readers will have a thorough understanding of how to build responsive user interfaces in Blazor Server applications using CSS. They will learn about various techniques for responsive design, including the use of CSS frameworks, media queries, and custom styling. Additionally, readers will gain insights into accessibility practices and the importance of thorough testing. With this knowledge, readers will be equipped to create visually appealing, user-friendly, and accessible applications that deliver a great experience across all devices.

Chapter 14: Implementing Authentication and Authorization in Blazor Server Applications

14.1 Introduction to Authentication and Authorization

In the modern web landscape, securing applications through effective authentication and authorization practices is paramount. Blazor Server applications often require user identity management to control access to certain features or content based on user roles and permissions.

- **Authentication**: The process of verifying the identity of a user. This can be done through various methods such as usernames and passwords, social logins, or multi-factor authentication.

- **Authorization**: Once a user is authenticated, authorization determines what resources the user can access and what actions they can perform.

This chapter will provide you with a comprehensive understanding of how to implement authentication and authorization in Blazor Server applications, using ASP.NET Core Identity and role-based access control.

14.2 Setting Up ASP.NET Core Identity

To handle user authentication and authorization, you need to set up ASP.NET Core Identity in your Blazor Server application. This section discusses the steps required to configure Identity.

Subtopics to Cover:

- **Installing Required Packages**: How to add ASP.NET Core Identity packages to your project.
- **Configuring Identity Services**: Registering Identity services in the Startup.cs file.
- **Creating User and Role Models**: Defining the user and role classes for your application.

Content Example:

1. **Installing Required Packages**: In your project's NuGet Package Manager, install the following packages:

```bash
Copy code
Install-Package Microsoft.AspNetCore.Identity.EntityFrameworkCore
Install-Package Microsoft.AspNetCore.
Authentication.Cookies
```

1. **Configuring Identity Services**: Update your Startup.cs to include Identity configuration:

```csharp
Copy code
public void ConfigureServices(IServiceCollection services)
{
    services.AddDbContext<ApplicationDbContext>(options =>
        options.UseSqlServer(Configuration.
GetConnectionString("DefaultConnection")));

    services.AddIdentity<IdentityUser, IdentityRole>()
```

```
    .AddEntityFrameworkStores<ApplicationDbContext>()
    .AddDefaultTokenProviders();

services.Configure<IdentityOptions>(options =>
{
    options.Password.RequireDigit = true;
    options.Password.RequiredLength = 6;
    options.Password.RequireNonAlphanumeric = false;
    options.Password.RequireUppercase = true;
    options.Password.RequireLowercase = true;
});

services.AddRazorPages();
services.AddServerSideBlazor();
}
```

1. **Creating User and Role Models**: You can customize the default user model by creating a new class that inherits from IdentityUser:

```csharp
Copy code
public class ApplicationUser : IdentityUser
{
    public string FirstName { get; set; }
    public string LastName { get; set; }
}
```

14.3 Implementing User Registration and Login

Once Identity is configured, you can implement user registration and login functionalities. This section guides you through creating the necessary UI components and backend logic.

Subtopics to Cover:

- **Creating the Registration Component**: Building a Blazor component for user registration that collects user details.

- **Implementing Registration Logic**: Writing the backend logic to create a new user account.
- **Creating the Login Component**: Building a component for user login, including input fields for credentials.

Content Example:

1. **Creating the Registration Component**:

```razor
Copy code
@page "/register"
@inject UserManager<ApplicationUser> UserManager
@inject NavigationManager Navigation

<EditForm Model="@user" OnValidSubmit="RegisterUser">
    <DataAnnotationsValidator />
    <ValidationSummary />

    <InputText id="username" @bind-Value="user.UserName"
    placeholder="Username" />
    <InputText id="email" @bind-Value="user.Email"
    placeholder="Email" />
    <InputText id="password" type="password"
    @bind-Value="password" placeholder="Password" />
    <InputText id="confirmPassword" type="password"
    @bind-Value="confirmPassword" placeholder="Confirm Password"
    />

    <button type="submit">Register</button>
</EditForm>

@code {
    private ApplicationUser user = new ApplicationUser();
    private string password;
    private string confirmPassword;
```

```
    private async Task RegisterUser()
    {
        if (password != confirmPassword)
        {
            // Show error message
            return;
        }

        var result = await UserManager.CreateAsync(user,
        password);
        if (result.Succeeded)
        {
            Navigation.NavigateTo("/login");
        }
    }
}
```

1. **Creating the Login Component**:

```razor
Copy code
@page "/login"
@inject SignInManager<ApplicationUser> SignInManager
@inject NavigationManager Navigation

<EditForm Model="@loginModel" OnValidSubmit="LoginUser">
    <DataAnnotationsValidator />
    <ValidationSummary />

    <InputText id="username" @bind-Value="loginModel.UserName"
    placeholder="Username" />
    <InputText id="password" type="password"
    @bind-Value="loginModel.Password" placeholder="Password" />

    <button type="submit">Login</button>
</EditForm>
```

```
@code {
    private LoginModel loginModel = new LoginModel();

    private async Task LoginUser()
    {
        var result = await
        SignInManager.PasswordSignInAsync(loginModel.UserName,
        loginModel.Password, isPersistent:
false, lockoutOnFailure: false);
        if (result.Succeeded)
        {
            Navigation.NavigateTo("/");
        }
        else
        {
            // Show error message
        }
    }

    public class LoginModel
    {
        public string UserName { get; set; }
        public string Password { get; set; }
    }
}
```

14.4 Implementing Logout Functionality

Providing a way for users to log out is essential for security and user experience. This section explains how to implement logout functionality in a Blazor Server application.

Subtopics to Cover:

- **Creating a Logout Component**: Building a simple component or button to handle user logout.
- **Implementing Logout Logic**: Writing the backend logic to sign out the user.

Content Example:

1. **Creating the Logout Component**:

```razor
Copy code
@page "/logout"
@inject SignInManager<ApplicationUser> SignInManager
@inject NavigationManager Navigation

@code {
    protected override async Task OnInitializedAsync()
    {
        await SignInManager.SignOutAsync();
        Navigation.NavigateTo("/");
    }
}
```

14.5 Role-Based Authorization

Role-based authorization allows you to restrict access to certain parts of your application based on user roles. This section will guide you through implementing role-based access control.

Subtopics to Cover:

- **Defining User Roles**: How to create roles in your application using ASP.NET Core Identity.
- **Assigning Roles to Users**: Writing the logic to assign roles to users during registration or through an admin interface.
- **Using [Authorize] Attribute**: Implementing the [Authorize] attribute to protect specific pages or components based on user roles.

Content Example:

1. **Defining User Roles**:

```csharp
Copy code
public async Task InitializeRoles(RoleManager<IdentityRole>
roleManager)
{
    string[] roleNames = { "Admin", "User" };
    foreach (var roleName in roleNames)
    {
        if (!await roleManager.RoleExistsAsync(roleName))
        {
            await roleManager.CreateAsync(new
            IdentityRole(roleName));
        }
    }
}
```

1. **Assigning Roles to Users**:

```csharp
Copy code
var user = await UserManager.
FindByEmailAsync("admin@example.com");
await UserManager.AddToRoleAsync(user, "Admin");
```

1. **Using the [Authorize] Attribute**:

```razor
Copy code
@page "/admin"
@attribute [Authorize(Roles = "Admin")]

<h3>Admin Page</h3>
```

14.6 Claims-Based Authorization

Claims-based authorization allows for more granular control over user access by evaluating specific user claims. This section discusses how to implement claims-based authorization in your Blazor Server application.

Subtopics to Cover:

- **Understanding Claims**: What claims are and how they differ from roles.
- **Adding Claims to Users**: How to add claims to users during registration or through an admin interface.
- **Using Claims in Authorization**: Implementing logic to check for specific claims in your application.

Content Example:

1. **Adding Claims to Users**:

```csharp
Copy code
await UserManager.AddClaimAsync(user, new Claim("CanEdit",
"true"));
```

1. **Using Claims for Authorization**:

```razor
Copy code
@page "/editor"
@attribute [Authorize(Policy = "CanEditPolicy")]

<h3>Editor Page</h3>
```

14.7 Customizing Authorization Policies

Custom authorization policies provide a powerful way to enforce complex security requirements. This section explains how to define and implement custom authorization policies in your Blazor Server application.

Subtopics to Cover:

- **Defining Authorization Policies**: How to create custom policies in Startup.cs.
- **Implementing Policy Requirements**: Writing classes that implement the IAuthorizationRequirement interface.
- **Using Policies in Your Application**: Applying custom policies to protect routes or components.

Content Example:

1. **Defining Authorization Policies**:

```csharp
Copy code
services.AddAuthorization(options =>
{
    options.AddPolicy("CanEditPolicy", policy =>
        policy.RequireClaim("CanEdit", "true"));
});
```

1. **Implementing Policy Requirements**:

```csharp
Copy code
public class CanEditRequirement : IAuthorizationRequirement
{
    // Custom logic
}
```

1. **Using Policies**:

```razor
Copy code
@page "/edit"
@attribute [Authorize(Policy = "CanEditPolicy")]

<h3>Edit Page</h3>
```

14.8 Securing APIs with Authentication and Authorization

When building APIs, securing them with authentication and authorization is essential. This section covers how to implement security measures for your APIs using JWT tokens.

Subtopics to Cover:

- **Implementing JWT Authentication**: How to set up JWT authentication for your API.
- **Generating JWT Tokens**: Writing logic to generate JWT tokens upon successful authentication.
- **Securing API Endpoints**: Applying the [Authorize] attribute to secure your API endpoints.

Content Example:

1. **Implementing JWT Authentication**:

```csharp
Copy code
services.AddAuthentication(JwtBearerDefaults.AuthenticationScheme)
        .AddJwtBearer(options =>
        {
            options.TokenValidationParameters = new
```

```
        TokenValidationParameters
        {
            ValidateIssuer = true,
            ValidateAudience = true,
            ValidateLifetime = true,
            ValidateIssuerSigningKey = true,
            ValidIssuer = Configuration["Jwt:Issuer"],
            ValidAudience = Configuration["Jwt:Audience"],
            IssuerSigningKey =
new SymmetricSecurityKey(Encoding.
UTF8.GetBytes(Configuration["Jwt:Key"]))
        };
    });
```

1. Generating JWT Tokens:

```csharp
Copy code
public string GenerateJwtToken(ApplicationUser user)
{
    var claims = new[]
    {
        new Claim(JwtRegisteredClaimNames.Sub, user.UserName),
        new Claim(JwtRegisteredClaimNames.Jti,
        Guid.NewGuid().ToString())
    };

    var key = new SymmetricSecurityKey(Encoding.UTF8.GetBytes
(Configuration["Jwt:Key"]));
    var creds = new SigningCredentials(key,
    SecurityAlgorithms.HmacSha256);

    var token = new JwtSecurityToken(
        issuer: Configuration["Jwt:Issuer"],
        audience: Configuration["Jwt:Audience"],
        claims: claims,
```

```
    expires: DateTime.Now.AddMinutes(30),
    signingCredentials: creds);

  return new JwtSecurityTokenHandler().WriteToken(token);
}
```

1. **Securing API Endpoints**:

```csharp
csharp
Copy code
[Authorize]
[HttpGet("secure-data")]
public IActionResult GetSecureData()
{
    return Ok("This is secure data.");
}
```

14.9 Testing Authentication and Authorization

Testing is essential to ensure that your authentication and authorization logic works as expected. This section discusses strategies for testing your authentication and authorization implementation.

Subtopics to Cover:

- **Unit Testing Authentication Logic**: How to write unit tests for your authentication methods.
- **Integration Testing for Secure APIs**: Testing your secure APIs to ensure they enforce authentication and authorization correctly.
- **User Acceptance Testing**: Conducting user acceptance testing to validate that authentication and authorization meet user expectations.

Content Example:

1. **Unit Testing Authentication Logic:**

```csharp
csharp
Copy code
[Fact]
public async Task Login_WithValidCredentials_ReturnsSuccess()
{
    var result = await _authService.Login("validUser",
    "validPassword");
    Assert.True(result.Succeeded);
}
```

1. **Integration Testing for Secure APIs:**

- Use tools like Postman to test API endpoints with and without authentication tokens.

1. **User Acceptance Testing:**

- Gather user feedback to ensure the authentication flow is intuitive and meets expectations.

14.10 Best Practices for Authentication and Authorization

Implementing robust authentication and authorization requires adhering to best practices to ensure security and user experience. This section outlines key recommendations for securing your Blazor Server applications.

Subtopics to Cover:

- **Use HTTPS**: Ensure that all communications are secured using HTTPS.
- **Implement Strong Password Policies**: Enforce strong password policies to protect user accounts.
- **Regularly Update Dependencies**: Keep your dependencies up-to-date to patch security vulnerabilities.

- **Monitor and Log Authentication Events**: Implement logging for authentication events to detect suspicious activities.

Content Example:

1. **Using HTTPS**:

- Configure your application to redirect all HTTP traffic to HTTPS.

1. **Strong Password Policies**:

```csharp
Copy code
options.Password.RequiredLength = 8;
options.Password.RequireDigit = true;
```

1. **Logging Authentication Events**:

```csharp
Copy code
public void Configure(IApplicationBuilder app, ILogger<Startup>
logger)
{
    app.Use(async (context, next) =>
    {
        logger.LogInformation("User Authentication: " +
        context.User.Identity.Name);
        await next.Invoke();
    });
}
```

Conclusion

By the end of Chapter 14, readers will have a comprehensive understanding of how to implement authentication and authorization in Blazor Server applications. They will learn about setting up ASP.NET Core Identity, creating user registration and login functionalities, managing roles and claims, securing APIs, and testing their implementation. With this knowledge, readers will be equipped to build secure Blazor applications that protect user data and manage access effectively.

Chapter 15: Advanced Blazor Server Techniques and Performance Optimization

15.1 Introduction to Advanced Techniques in Blazor Server

As you become more proficient with Blazor Server, you may want to explore advanced techniques that can enhance your application's functionality and performance. This chapter will cover a range of advanced topics, including state management, component communication, and performance optimization techniques.

- **Why Advanced Techniques Matter**: Leveraging advanced features and techniques allows developers to build more efficient, maintainable, and scalable applications. This can significantly improve user experience and application performance.

15.2 State Management in Blazor Server

Managing application state effectively is crucial for building responsive and interactive Blazor applications. This section discusses various state management strategies you can implement in your Blazor Server applications.

Subtopics to Cover:

- **Understanding State Management**: An overview of state management concepts in web applications.

- **Using Cascading Parameters**: How to pass data down the component tree efficiently.
- **Utilizing the StateContainer Pattern**: Implementing a shared state management solution across components.
- **Blazor's Built-In State Management Features**: Overview of built-in features for state management in Blazor.

Content Example:

1. **Understanding State Management**:

- State can refer to any data that needs to persist across different user interactions, such as user preferences, authentication status, or temporary data during a session.

1. **Using Cascading Parameters**:

```razor
Copy code
@code {
    [CascadingParameter]
    public AppState AppState { get; set; }
}
```

1. **Utilizing the StateContainer Pattern**:

```csharp
Copy code
public class StateContainer
{
```

```
public event Action OnChange;
private string _someData;

public string SomeData
{
    get => _someData;
    set
    {
        _someData = value;
        NotifyStateChanged();
    }
}

private void NotifyStateChanged() => OnChange?.Invoke();
}
```

15.3 Component Communication Techniques

In a Blazor Server application, components often need to communicate with each other to share data and trigger events. This section covers several techniques for effective component communication.

Subtopics to Cover:

- **Parameter Binding**: Passing data between parent and child components using parameters.
- **EventCallback for Parent-Child Communication**: Using EventCallback to handle events in parent components.
- **Service-Based Communication**: Implementing services for communication between components that are not directly related.
- **Using Interfaces for Loose Coupling**: Creating interfaces to facilitate communication between components.

Content Example:

1. **Parameter Binding**:

```razor
razor
Copy code
<ChildComponent SomeParameter="parentData" />
```

1. EventCallback:

```razor
razor
Copy code
<button @onclick="() => OnClicked.InvokeAsync()">Click Me</button>
```

1. Service-Based Communication:

```csharp
csharp
Copy code
public class NotificationService
{
    public event Action NotificationReceived;

    public void Notify() => NotificationReceived?.Invoke();
}
```

1. Using Interfaces:

```csharp
csharp
Copy code
public interface INotificationService
{
    void Notify(string message);
```

```
}
```

15.4 Handling Forms and Validation

Forms are a critical part of many web applications. This section discusses advanced techniques for handling forms and implementing validation in Blazor Server applications.

Subtopics to Cover:

- **Building Complex Forms**: How to create and manage complex forms with nested components.
- **Custom Validation Attributes**: Implementing custom validation logic for form fields.
- **Integrating Third-Party Validation Libraries**: Using libraries like FluentValidation for advanced validation scenarios.

Content Example:

1. **Building Complex Forms**:

```razor
Copy code
<EditForm Model="@model" OnValidSubmit="HandleValidSubmit">
    <DataAnnotationsValidator />
    <ValidationSummary />
    <InputText id="name" @bind-Value="model.Name" />
    <AddressComponent Address="@model.Address" />
    <button type="submit">Submit</button>
</EditForm>
```

1. **Custom Validation Attributes**:

```csharp
Copy code
public class MyCustomValidationAttribute : ValidationAttribute
{
    protected override ValidationResult IsValid(object value,
    ValidationContext validationContext)
    {
        // Custom validation logic
        return ValidationResult.Success;
    }
}
```

1. **Integrating FluentValidation**:

```csharp
Copy code
services.AddFluentValidation(fv =>
fv.RegisterValidatorsFromAssemblyContaining<Startup>());
```

15.5 Performance Optimization Techniques

Optimizing the performance of your Blazor Server application is critical for delivering a fast and responsive user experience. This section covers various techniques for enhancing performance.

Subtopics to Cover:

- **Reducing Component Render Time**: Techniques for minimizing the rendering time of components.
- **Lazy Loading Components**: Implementing lazy loading to improve initial load times.
- **Using Virtualization for Large Lists**: How to use virtualization for efficiently rendering large lists.
- **Minifying and Bundling Assets**: Strategies for minifying and bundling CSS and JavaScript files.

Content Example:

1. **Reducing Component Render Time**:

- Optimize rendering by using ShouldRender method to control when a component should re-render.

1. **Lazy Loading Components**:

```razor
Copy code
@if (isLoaded)
{
    <MyComponent />
}
else
{
    <LoadingComponent />
}
```

1. **Using Virtualization**:

```razor
Copy code
<Virtualize Items="@items" ItemSize="50">
    <ItemTemplate>
        <div>@context</div>
    </ItemTemplate>
</Virtualize>
```

1. **Minifying and Bundling**:

- Use tools like WebOptimizer or build pipeline tasks to bundle and minify your assets.

15.6 Caching Strategies for Blazor Server Applications

Caching can greatly improve the performance of your Blazor Server applications by reducing the need to retrieve data repeatedly. This section discusses caching strategies you can implement.

Subtopics to Cover:

- **In-Memory Caching**: How to use in-memory caching to store frequently accessed data.
- **Distributed Caching**: Implementing distributed caching solutions like Redis for scalability.
- **Client-Side Caching with HTTP Cache**: Techniques for leveraging HTTP caching to improve performance.

Content Example:

1. **In-Memory Caching**:

```csharp
Copy code
services.AddMemoryCache();
```

1. **Distributed Caching with Redis**:

```csharp
Copy code
services.AddStackExchangeRedisCache(options =>
{
```

```
    options.Configuration = "localhost:6379";
});
```

1. **Client-Side Caching**:

- Use cache control headers in your API responses to instruct browsers to cache data.

15.7 Testing and Debugging Blazor Server Applications

Effective testing and debugging practices are vital for maintaining application quality. This section discusses tools and strategies for testing and debugging Blazor Server applications.

Subtopics to Cover:

- **Unit Testing Blazor Components**: Techniques for writing unit tests for your Blazor components.
- **Integration Testing**: Writing tests that cover the interactions between components and services.
- **Debugging Techniques**: Tools and methods for debugging Blazor applications effectively.

Content Example:

1. **Unit Testing Blazor Components**:

```csharp
csharp
Copy code
[Fact]
public void Component_ShouldRenderCorrectly()
{
    var component = RenderComponent<MyComponent>();
```

```
    component.MarkupMatches("<div>Hello, World!</div>");
}
```

1. **Integration Testing**:

- Use test servers to simulate full application behavior during integration tests.

1. **Debugging Techniques**:

- Leverage the browser's developer tools for debugging and performance monitoring.

15.8 Internationalization (i18n) and Localization (l10n)

Internationalization and localization are essential for building applications that cater to users in different regions and languages. This section discusses how to implement i18n and l10n in Blazor Server applications.

Subtopics to Cover:

- **Understanding i18n and l10n**: Definitions and importance of i18n and l10n.
- **Setting Up Localization in Blazor**: How to configure localization in your Blazor Server application.
- **Creating and Managing Resource Files**: Techniques for managing language-specific resource files.

Content Example:

1. **Setting Up Localization**: In Startup.cs:

```csharp
Copy code
services.AddLocalization(options => options.ResourcesPath =
"Resources");
```

1. **Creating Resource Files**: Create a resource file named Resources.resx for default language strings and Resources.es.resx for Spanish.
2. **Using Localization in Components**:

```razor
Copy code
@inject IStringLocalizer<Resources> localizer

<h1>@localizer["WelcomeMessage"]</h1>
```

15.9 Integrating Client-Side Libraries

Blazor Server allows you to integrate client-side JavaScript libraries, providing additional functionality to your application. This section discusses how to incorporate JavaScript libraries in your Blazor projects.

Subtopics to Cover:

- **Adding JavaScript Libraries**: How to include JavaScript libraries in your project.
- **Interoperability with JavaScript**: Techniques for calling JavaScript functions from Blazor components and vice versa.
- **Using Popular Libraries**: Examples of using libraries like jQuery, Chart.js, or D3.js in your Blazor applications.

Content Example:

1. **Adding JavaScript Libraries**: Include the library in _Host.cshtml:

```
html
Copy code
<script
src="https://code.jquery.com/jquery-3.6.0.min.js"></script>
```

1. **Interoperability with JavaScript**:

```csharp
csharp
Copy code
[Inject] IJSRuntime JSRuntime { get; set; }

private async Task CallJsFunction()
{
    await JSRuntime.InvokeVoidAsync("myJsFunction", parameter);
}
```

1. **Using Chart.js**: Create a JavaScript function to render charts and call it from your Blazor component.
2. **10 Preparing for Production**

Once you've implemented advanced techniques and optimizations, preparing your Blazor Server application for production is essential. This section covers the final steps for a successful deployment.

Subtopics to Cover:

- **Final Testing and Validation**: Conducting thorough testing before going live.
- **Performance Monitoring Post-Deployment**: Setting up tools for monitoring performance after deployment.
- **User Feedback and Continuous Improvement**: Establishing a feed-

back loop to gather user input and continuously improve your application.

Content Example:

1. **Final Testing and Validation**:

- Perform load testing and user acceptance testing to ensure readiness for production.

1. **Performance Monitoring**: Integrate tools like Application Insights for ongoing monitoring.
2. **User Feedback Mechanisms**:

- Implement features for collecting user feedback, such as surveys or in-app feedback forms.

Conclusion

By the end of Chapter 15, readers will have a comprehensive understanding of advanced techniques in Blazor Server applications and strategies for optimizing performance. They will learn about state management, component communication, performance optimization, authentication, localization, and integrating client-side libraries. With this knowledge, readers will be equipped to enhance their Blazor applications, ensuring they are efficient, secure, and ready for production deployment.

Conclusion

As we conclude this journey through building and deploying Blazor Server applications, it's important to reflect on the comprehensive skills and knowledge you have acquired. Blazor Server, as a powerful web framework, enables developers to create rich, interactive web applications using C# and .NET, breaking traditional barriers and allowing for a more cohesive development experience.

Key Takeaways

Throughout this book, we have explored a wide range of topics essential for mastering Blazor Server. Here are some of the key takeaways:

Understanding Blazor Fundamentals: We began with an introduction to Blazor Server, understanding its architecture, components, and lifecycle. You learned how Blazor allows for real-time web applications with a server-side rendering model, leveraging the power of .NET on the server while delivering rich UI interactions in the browser.

Routing and Navigation: You gained insights into routing and navigation within Blazor applications, learning to define routes and manage navigation state. The ability to build seamless user experiences through effective routing is crucial for any web application.

Data Management: Implementing APIs and managing data effectively were central themes. You explored how to build and consume APIs, implement CRUD operations, and handle data binding in Blazor, ensuring that your applications can interact with various data sources efficiently.

Authentication and Authorization: Security is paramount in modern applications. This book covered how to implement robust authentication and authorization using ASP.NET Core Identity, allowing you to secure your applications and manage user access with confidence.

Responsive Design: The importance of building responsive user interfaces cannot be overstated. You learned how to leverage CSS, CSS frameworks, and responsive design principles to create applications that provide excellent user experiences across all devices.

Advanced Techniques: We delved into advanced topics such as state management, component communication, performance optimization, and integration with client-side libraries. These skills will empower you to build sophisticated applications that meet the needs of users in dynamic environments.

Deployment and Maintenance: Finally, we covered the critical steps in deploying your Blazor Server applications to various hosting environments. You learned how to prepare your application for production, implement CI/CD practices, and monitor application performance post-deployment to ensure a smooth user experience.

The Road Ahead

While this book provides a solid foundation in Blazor Server development, the field of web development is constantly evolving. Here are a few suggestions for your continued learning and growth:

Explore Advanced Features: Blazor is continually updated with new features and improvements. Stay current by exploring the official Microsoft documentation, community forums, and GitHub repositories for the latest advancements in Blazor.

Build Real-World Projects: The best way to solidify your understanding is through hands-on experience. Create real-world projects that challenge you to apply what you've learned. Whether it's a personal project or contributing to open-source, practical application reinforces theoretical knowledge.

Engage with the Community: The Blazor community is vibrant and supportive. Participate in community discussions, attend meetups or webinars, and engage with other developers to share experiences and learn from one another.

Expand Your Skill Set: Consider branching out into related areas such as Blazor WebAssembly for client-side applications, or learning about microservices architecture and containerization with Docker. The broader your skill set, the more versatile you become as a developer.

Final Thoughts

In summary, Blazor Server represents a significant step forward in web development, providing a seamless and efficient way to build interactive applications. By harnessing the power of C# and .NET, developers can create applications that are not only powerful but also maintainable and scalable.

Your journey with Blazor Server has equipped you with the skills necessary to navigate this exciting technology. As you move forward, remember that learning is a continuous process. Embrace challenges, seek knowledge, and keep building. Your journey as a Blazor developer is just beginning, and the possibilities are limitless.

Thank you for embarking on this journey with us. We wish you great success in your Blazor Server development endeavors!